CANADIAN
MANTLES
OF REVIVAL

Sara Maynard

Cover design by Ryan Tsuen.

ISBN: 1505355303
ISBN 13: 9781505355307

Dedication

This is for you, Jesus.

Your fame is the desire of my heart. May you shine through these pages, and may your people have more reasons than ever to love you with abandon, boast loudly about your glorious grace, and pursue you like no other generation ever has.

Thank-yous

To Cyndy d'Entremont, Tanya Bellhumeur-Allatt and Brant Levert – you each sowed life-giving encouragement and superb coaching that brought this project to completion. It wouldn't have happened without you. Thank you so much.

To Mike and the tribe: You will always be my heroes. Thank you for your patience and grace with my intensity, your love, laughter, protection, and unflinching support.

To the Redleaf team: It's a tremendous honour to run with such a godly, sold-out team who loves Jesus with full abandon and contends daily for a great revival in the nation! Your vision, sacrifice and passion always call me higher.

Endorsements

"There are some who carry the heart for their family, some their people, even others an entire city. But there are few who really carry God's heart for an entire nation. When you meet them, hear them, even at times merely read them, you are "moved upon" to take a stand. These standard bearers are often called ambassadors or patriots and sometimes others refer to them as "statesmen or stateswomen". They inspire you. Impact you. And you? Well, you hear a sound of a call to take action! One of these unassuming voices on the rise, she is the author of the book you are now holding; Sara Maynard with Redleaf Ministries, for the healing of the land called Canada. It is with deep respect and honor that commend to you the life, ministry and writings of this stateswomen for such a time as this."

Dr. James W Goll
Encounters Network • Prayer Storm • Compassion Acts
International Best Selling Author

"I have read Sara's book with growing interest at every page. It has sparked a fire in my heart beyond what I expected. Not only has she done a great job relating the stories of past revivals, but also the lessons she draws from them are invaluable. Great revelatory teaching! We can feel the revival mantle hovering all over the book. I am truly impressed and deeply impacted."

Alain Caron
Author, Apostolic Centers
Leader of the Hodos network

"There are seasons in life when you carry a specific assignment from heaven. You know it by strategic timing, connection with special people and key insights opened up to you. This book about Canadian mantles and revivals is Sara's assignment. It pieces together Canadian revival history in a way never captured before. It then sets the stage for what many believe will see Canada playing a prominent role in an end time revival prior to the second coming of Christ. I predict that this book will be known in the years ahead as contributing significantly to Canadian and worldwide revival history."

Pastor Doug A. Schneider
The Embassy Church
Oshawa, Ontario, Canada

"I've heard it said, 'History belongs to the intercessor'. Since our Heavenly Father is writing His Story in Canada, a nation destined for spiritual, economic, and leadership greatness in the last days, He is raising up a powerful praying army. One of Canada's champion generals in this army is Sara Maynard. Tirelessly traversing our nation raising awareness of the prophetic destiny of this great land and sounding the banner cry to pray and fast in agreement with God's plan, Sara has been a national leader for many years.

In *Canadian Mantles of Revival*, Sara has penned a work destined to be a Canadian classic. She weaves stories of Canada's rich spiritual history with the call to stand in prayer and fasting for future nation wide revival. This fascinating book will raise hunger for more of God and motivate action to see His purposes fulfilled. Indeed it is now our time and our watch. Let us run this race for the prize set before us personally and nationally - Jesus Christ and His fullness on earth."

Reverend Patricia Bootsma
Co Lead Pastor Catch the Fire Toronto Airport
Leader Catch the Fire Toronto House of Prayer

Director Ontario Prophetic Counsel
Author and Itinerant Speaker

"Prayer and revival are two dynamics that bring one's heart closer to God! Sara has done and excellent job in interfacing these two most important topics into a common thread. She has left us with a wellspring of faith and hope for our personal lives, the Church, and our nation. Your spirit will be stirred as you read these pages of fire and faith."

Dr. George D. Johnson
Convening Apostolic Leader for the
Canadian Coalition of Apostolic Leaders &
George Johnson Ministries International

"I commend Sara's new book. We need people like Sara to keep us from being weary in well doing. She reminds us that God has brought revival before to Canada, and he will do it again. May we not miss what God is doing!"

The Rev Dr Ed Hird, Rector
St. Simon's Church North Vancouver
Best selling author

"My heart burned within me as I read *Canadian Mantles of Revival*. This is a now word and a must read for anyone with a heart for revival in Canada. It is not only historically Informative but instructive, inspiring, and full of tangible impartation. These pages contain a part of our national inheritance. May we take up the charge to arise with fervent faith and prayer, as former generations have, to see the fullness of God's promises sweep Canada from sea to sea!

Thank you Sara Maynard for this powerful compilation and compelling call."

Faytene Grasseschi,
TheCRY Movement & MY Canada Association

"*Canadian Mantles of Revival* is a must read for the Body of Christ in Canada and especially for those who desire to see a needed 'move of God' in our nation. In Sara's book we are reminded that God has done it before and He can do it again as we align ourselves with those who have gone before us.

This is not only a refreshing read of how various revivals have touched different parts of our nation, but Sara has also included wonderful and valuable teachings on the prayerful posture that is needed to see new breakthroughs of revival in Canada. I can testify that Sara is not writing from a place of theory, but from years of tried, tested, and true experience combined with a heart filled with a desire to equip the Canadian Church for the days we are now living in."

Rob Parker
Founder and Director
National House of Prayer

Table of Contents

Forward

I can think of no better person to write a book on the history of revival in Canada than Sara Maynard. Sara is a true Canadian. For as long as I have known her, she has loved our nation and given herself to see Canada fulfill the purposes for which God has established it. The reader will have confidence in knowing that all of the things you will read about in this book for revival to come to a nation, Sara herself has done. She has prayed in secret, she has gathered multitudes to pray, she has fasted, she has humbled herself, she has soaked, abided, persevered – you name it, she has given her life to see national revival.

For all you Canadian readers, you will take delight in reading the incredible spiritual history of our great nation. God has chosen Canada to be the flashpoint of several worldwide revivals. The oldest spiritual colony in North America is found in Canada and we have been a birthplace of moves of God ever since. For all you international readers, you may be surprised to discover that, though we are small in terms of population, God has used the Canadian Church to spread revival to the four corners of the globe. From our history, you will understand our destiny — to be a "leaf of healing to the nations."

I am honoured to recommend this book to you. You will not only learn history, you will also learn the principles that almost always precede a great outpouring of the Holy Spirit. You will become hungry for the "greater works" that Jesus spoke of. Desire for more of God will be stirred in your heart. I pray you will ultimately be moved to imitate the faith of these great Canadian revivalists so that the Lord may also use you to bring Him the nations for His inheritance (Psalm 2:8)

Stacey Campbell
Pastor/Author
Beahero.org

Introduction

CANADIAN MANTLES OF REVIVAL

———

Pastor Bob Birch was a small man who always looked quite frail. As the pastor of a modest, traditional congregation at St. Margaret's Reformed Episcopalian Church on the east side of Vancouver, he led a quiet life- quiet, that is, until he encountered the power of the Holy Spirit through the ministry of Dennis Bennett, the minister at St. Luke's Episcopalian in Seattle. From that time on until his passing, a few weeks short of his hundredth birthday, Pastor Bob became one of the key fathers for the Jesus People Movement and a mighty apostle of prayer in the nation. Pastor Bob lived in a spirit of revival. In his later years, he travelled the nation, crisscrossing back and forth, calling the church to prayer, to intimacy with Jesus, to holiness, and to unity.

Pastor Bob was a spiritual father to my husband, Mike, and me, who were saved through his ministry and mentored by his example. His life and legacy are of a friend and servant of the Lord, but also, a spiritual pioneer in our land.

Bob Birch, as well as other men and women God has used in revival throughout the history of Canada, has left an inheritance, even a mantle, to pass to those that follow behind in future generations—if we will pick it up.

What is this mantle, and how do we step into it? It is more than just a vague sense of echo from the past, manifesting in the current generation, like the shape of a nose or a mannerism that pops up through the genes in random generations. It's more than an impartation or anointing that we might gain from a pilgrimage to gravesites of our nation's revivalists and a short time of prayer.

No, it's a mantle that comes by walking in the same spirit and being discipled by the lives of our forefathers. There is so much that can be learned and so much that we can receive from past generations, which means we don't have to discover or pioneer everything ourselves.

"And he said to them, "'Therefore every scribe who has been trained for the kingdom of heaven is like a master of a house, who brings out of his treasure what is new and what is old.'" Matthew 13:52 ESV

"Hear, O sons, a father's instruction, and be attentive, that you may gain insight..." Proverbs 4:1

The lives and testimonies of past revivalists continually inspire and challenge the Church, and so they should. The story of David Brainard's short life, for example, has propelled countless men and women into the mission field; William Carey even considered it a sacred text. Diaries and journals, penned through the years, have recorded the fire, the sacrifice, and the glory of revival for us to treasure like family jewels. Our forefathers' stories of pressing into God, living in a zealous love for Him, overcoming opposition, and enduring suffering with their eyes on the prize inspire us and give us courage for our modest struggles.

The accounts of the manifest presence of God, overwhelming a region with grace and conviction so that souls stream to the cross and whole cities are transformed, continually capture the heart and vision of the Church. They never grow old or threadbare. They keep us hungry, pull us into prayer, lift our faith, and steady our commitment to see revival flow throughout Canada or many other nations. This is the power of testimony.

Canada's Testimonies

However, when revival stories are told, it's rare to see the stories of our nation featured. In fact I'm increasingly aware that they are scarcely known. Everyone has heard the testimonies of Azusa Street, the Welsh Revival, the Second Great Awakening in America, but when I minister in different parts of Canada and do an impromptu poll of who has heard of Henry Alline, Phoebe Palmer, or the Sutera Twins, two or three hands may rise in a room full of two hundred or more people.

It seems like our heritage and testimonies have been obscured from our collective memory, and because of that, so many Canadian Christians believe our land has been spiritually stunted. Yet, in fact, the opposite is true—there is fruit everywhere! We have a rich heritage, not just in the founding of our nation but in the regular moves of God that have been poured out in Canada, touching, at some point, every region of this vast nation.

There are three compelling reasons that the recapturing of our Canadian revival history, our stories and testimonies, is so vital, especially in this hour:

1) So we can turn our hearts to our fathers and walk in what they spiritually apprehended

2) So we can be built up in faith

3) So we can align with the living prayers of those that have pioneered in revival, and as we unite in agreement, gain the greatest breakthroughs our nation has ever known

Let's look at each of these a bit closer.

Turning Our Hearts to Our Fathers:

My ancestors were men and women who pioneered in the early years of this nation. They were mostly simple people, seeking a better life for their families, doing what was necessary and at times paying a great cost. My mother's great-great grandfather, John Spencer, originally from Huguenot stock, came as a United Empire Loyalist and settled in Cape Breton, Nova Scotia. There, he and his wife actively joined in the pioneer community and contributed to see it grow and develop.

My father's grandfather, Peter McAra, son of a corporal in the British Army, came to Canada as a child when his father left the army and the family emigrated from Scotland. They came for the promise of free land, which was being offered to the brave ones who would homestead on the prairies.

His father, Peter Sr. built a sod hut, where they spent their first Saskatchewan winter, along with his mother and seven siblings. They had no roads, hospitals, schools, few stores or friends, and had left their extended family behind. Pioneering means you build and establish both infrastructure and community, so those coming after you don't have to.

I think of this at times when I'm in Saskatchewan and pick up a cell signal to guide me, while travelling on a well-paved road, between the vibrant cities in the province. It makes me thankful for those who went ahead and made a way for us to follow.

A Promise for This Hour

One of the prophetic promises that has been repeatedly highlighted by the Holy Spirit as key for this generation is the promise of Malachi 4:5,6, the last promise of the Old Testament.

"Behold, I will send you Elijah the prophet before the great and awesome day of the Lord comes. And he will turn the hearts of fathers to their children and the hearts of children to their fathers, lest I come and strike the land with a decree of utter destruction."

This promise contains the vision of fathers and children with hearts turned toward each other in agreement, harmony, and honour. What was begun by the Lord in the lives of the fathers of our nation, especially in the realm of revival, rolls through the generations, increasing in fullness. As we now turn our heart toward our fathers, their teaching and mantles, we can be truly discipled by them, rather than having to pioneer our own independent way.

But how do you have your heart turned toward the forefathers of revival if you don't even know who they were or what they wrestled for? How do you agree with them if you only know sketchy details about their lives, but never glimpse into their hearts? Because this promise is so alive for us right now, it's absolutely critical we find out about the Canadian fathers and mothers of revival and learn from their lives, their prayers, and their passion. Most of these are a part of the great cloud of witnesses, yet we can be tutored by their legacy—what they left behind to assist us to run farther and faster.

This is a golden opportunity that the Father has opened up for us. We can have our "hearts turned to our fathers" through humbly learning and honouring our roots and the spiritual DNA of revival in this nation. We can learn from any nation, and so we should, for there is only one Body of Christ. Yet God has appointed the times and places for all men to live, and this nation has a unique, vibrant history of revival that puts a special responsibility of stewardship on the shoulders of Canadian Christians. We have a responsibility to spread this revival DNA both to our generation and to pass it on to future generations.

As we find out about what was apprehended spiritually by our forefathers, we can pick up their mantles, run in them, and pass them on in even greater fullness to those of the next generation, who are rising up with faith and fire.

Built Up in Faith

Because prayer stands head and shoulders above every other factor as the most consistent and critical contributor to revival, we want to do everything we can to nurture prayer in our lives, our homes, churches, and country. Our God hears and answers prayer! I serve full time as the director of Redleaf Prayer, and as a ministry, this is one of the prime mandates that we give ourselves to—the call to awaken and mobilize prayer in Canada. But our call is not just to awaken all forms of prayer, but specifically prayer that births revival.

As I've travelled serving this vision, I've yet to run into a believer that says prayer doesn't matter or prayer is not answered. We all theologically believe in prayer, yet prayerlessness continues to be rampant. The corporate prayer meeting is so often the least attended of meetings in the church's calendar, and a personal prayer life is often not much more that a quick blessing of the food at meal time. So if we have heaven's resources at our disposal for the asking... , why don't we ask?

I believe the most pervasive reason is we personally don't live in the experience of answered prayer. While we believe God answers and have had some experience with our prayers being answered, it's not an everyday reality, and in its absence, unbelief has crept in. Unbelief is the greatest killer of prayer. The writer of Hebrews says it like this:

"And without faith it is impossible to please him, for whoever would draw near to God must believe that he exists and that he rewards those who seek him." Hebrews 11:6

If we don't believe He rewards those that pursue Him nor responds to our heartfelt cries, why would we pray? So it becomes apparent that faith is the vital missing piece in many, if not most, lives, and we must do whatever we can to encourage the growth of faith in our walk with God. The result of faith mixed with desire is fervent, prevailing prayer, the very dynamo of revival.

Andrew Murray shares this conviction of our need for faith, stating: "Faith in a prayer-hearing God will make a prayer-loving Christian."

When Redleaf holds schools of prayer, we frequently teach on what builds up faith and also how to watch for the things that undermine faith. It's vital that we intentionally choose faith and proactively seek to strengthen our faith. We'll delve into some of that teaching in a later chapter, but for now we can be aware that a massive contributor to faith being built is the power of testimony.

This is one of the primary reasons why we are recounting the history of so many of our nation's revivals in this book—so we can rise in faith. It's the knowledge of what has transpired on this land with previous generations of Canadians, which makes believing for an even greater move of God so much easier.

Adding Our Prayers

One of the most important seasons of learning in the ministry of prayer for me was the four years I served as director of the Vancouver House of Prayer. As the first house of prayer in the nation, our little team was full of passion and enthusiasm but utterly lacking in experience. Vision was strong, but even among the very supportive pastors in the region, we were unaware of anyone who had gone this way before. We were pioneering and following the cloud through the wilderness.

While this certainly wasn't the easiest season of ministry, I wouldn't trade it for anything. The lessons God taught us and the miracles he did in our midst have been an invaluable foundation for all prayer ministry I've been involved with since. However, at the end of that season, the Lord clearly spoke to us, through a national prophet, that it was time to close the doors. I was completely shocked, as we had finally broken through on a number of levels, and it looked like we were poised to grow with strength.

Arguing with God clearly wasn't changing His mind or His word to us, so surrender was the only option. But in those days, it seemed like a great defeat—like all we had build at such a great cost was now going to be lost. "Not so," the Lord said to me, "for all the prayers that has been prayed in these four years—all these thousands of prayers—remain before me. These, which were filled with faith and lined up with my heart, will bear fruit. It's just a matter of time."

Suddenly I was reminded and aware in a fresh way that the work was the work of prayer, not the outward building of a structure that hosted prayer. And Spirit led prayer itself had no "best before" stamp on it.

One of the most frequent prayers we prayed during those four years was for houses of prayer to spring up all over Canada. We would look out the east window, stretching out our hands in intercession. Our prayer was for them to be birthed, for them to thrive and fill the land with a spirit of prayer. Today, it's a thrill to walk with leaders from the over twenty-three houses of prayer spread across the nation, as well as dozens of other prayer networks and ministries, which all began subsequent to the Vancouver House of Prayer. Did we pray them into being? Yes and no. Yes, our prayers contributed (maybe powerfully so), but no, we, of course, weren't alone in that. Countless others prayed as well. As in almost all answers to prayer, we played a part in seeing the answer come—but only a part. Knowing this ensures Jesus gets all the glory.

What is now exciting to see is that many of these houses of prayer and prayer networks consistently pray for the Canadian prayer movement; they also pray for new houses of prayer to be launched and strengthened. Everything has multiplied. Each of these houses of prayer is carrying burdens for our nation to grow in righteousness, for the Church to mature and for souls to be saved. The incense of prayer is rapidly multiplying and filing the land.

Every generation has a call to fulfill the purposes of God for their time, and a part of that is adding their prayers to the prayers of their forefathers so that the cry for the increase of the kingdom is never silenced. Rather, like the story of praying for the Canadian prayer movement, it multiplies from many voices. Jesus Himself set in motion intergenerational agreement that has rolled through the history of the Church. The Church has always agreed with Him in prayer for an increase of His kingdom. With all of this historical momentum and agreement snowballing behind us, as we turn our hearts to our fathers, we can be confident that the greatest breakthroughs and demonstrations of the kingdom are yet to come.

"From the time of John the Baptizer until now, the kingdom of heaven has been forcefully advancing, and forceful people have been seizing it." [1]Matthew 11:12

"Of the increase of his government and of peace, there will be no end..." Isaiah 9:7a

Fruit Continues to Increase

While the intensity of the moves of God recorded in this book have waned, their fruit—the lives redeemed, the salvations, the restored marriages, the encounters, the healings and miracles that came through the original revivals—has continued to grow and impact our nation and many others. They are like concentric circles as one life touches another, which touches another and then another with the love of God, rippling from the epicentre of revival. The kingdom of heaven is like a mustard seed in the garden that grows to be the biggest plant, its supernatural influence is unstoppable.

"He put another parable before them, saying, 'The kingdom of heaven is like a grain of mustard seed that a man took and sowed in his field. It is the smallest of all seeds, but when it has grown it is larger than all the garden plants and becomes a tree, so that the birds of the air come and make nests in its branches.'

He told them another parable. 'The kingdom of heaven is like leaven that a woman took and hid in three measures of flour, till it was all leavened.'" Matthew 13:31–33

Even as we consider these revivals and the impact they have had upon the spiritual life of our nation, it's hard to imagine there are any

Canadian Christians who have not in some way benefited by what God did through our revivals. Surely everyone can trace the source of some blessing in their lives back to one of these moves of God, and of course, for some the impact has been massive. It's been utter, glorious transformation. It's been from death to life.

Yet the labours of our forefathers were not complete, especially in the realm of prayer. Their passionate, faith-filled prayers stand, as yours and mine do, before the throne of God, waiting for the fullness of the answer to be released. What they touched in their time, we can see increase in ours, if we will turn our hearts to learn from them.

If our prayers are Spirit led, Bible based, and infused with faith, we add to their prayers and agree with them for the same heavenly vision that they saw.

The bowls of heaven continue to be filled with the prayers of the saints, even if some of those prayers were prayed by saints long passed away and are now a part of the great cloud of witnesses. The Lord Jesus has not changed in His vision for this nation.

His vision is the kingdom coming to Canada as it is in heaven. This vision is like a mighty river, flowing from the cross through history, getting deeper and stronger all the time. It's important we know we are a part of this great company and not an independent generation adrift in the ocean of history.

So this book is about many of our nation's revivals, key times that God has moved and swept into the nation, changing everything. But it's also about some of the principles and lessons we can learn from the legacy of revival we've inherited. We don't have to build all our own roads or dig all our own wells. Much of the path has been forged for us by the spiritual pioneers in revival, and if we are humble and teachable, we can benefit greatly. We have dear fathers and mothers in revival, with much to pass on to us for this time.

Let's then consider the prayers of Pastor Bill McLeod, the preaching of Hugh Crossley, and the labours of Henry Alline. Let's invite fresh faith and vision of a revived Canada into our hearts. Let's embrace the same burden for revival in prayer that consumed those from previous generations and moved the heart of God so deeply. Let's welcome these eternal sounds of revival that our forefathers birthed back into our nation and see them come again with multiplied harvest, holiness, glory, and fire.

Chapter 1

What Is Revival?

———

Before we get to the stories, let's clarify a bit more precisely what we mean by "revival," so we can all be on the same page. In recent days this word *revival* has been used in a wide variety of ways. We hear about a spirit of revival, a revival culture, revivalists, personal revival, and so forth. There is no wrong usage, but the wide variety of usage has brought quite a bit of confusion. So whenever we speak or write about revival, it's helpful to define how we're using the word.

In this book, we're calling revival the phenomenon of a visitation of the manifest presence of God upon a church, a region, or a people to the point that His nearness and His direct working in hearts impacts the spiritual climate with many of the following changes:

- restored life of the Spirit in the Church
- a glorious revelation of Christ, fresh and clear in every heart
- the fear of the Lord
- extravagant worship
- fiery, extended, widespread prayer
- widespread conviction of sin, resulting in repentance, and a new love of holiness
- renewed commitments to God by backsliders and prodigals
- great awakening and hunger for spiritual things by the general population

- huge numbers of salvations
- release of the power of God
- supernatural signs and miracles
- heightened awareness of the spiritual realities of heaven and hell
- restored passion for the lost in the Church
- reconciliation of relationships and growth of unity
- controversy and opposition
- a fresh commitment to foreign missions

Now, do all of these occur in every revival? No, not at all. But the majority will be featured in each revival as they are the consistent symptoms of a community being impacted by God's presence. This is what happens to us when God comes near.

The end result, historically and biblically, of the work of God in revival is a wholesale change of the spiritual climate of a region, bringing tremendous growth in the Church and then following on, if it's not aborted, pervasive societal transformation.

The marking features of historic revivals have been humility, hunger, awakening, but above all, prayer—not just casual prayer, but deep groaning, travailing, persevering prayer, as Charles Finney calls it, "prevailing prayer." D.L. Moody said it simply: "Every great move of God can be traced to a kneeling figure."

National Revival

Although Canada has had some amazing and glorious revivals in our nation's history, national revival still has not yet swept across our land to light up the whole nation with God's glory coast to coast. This is one of the great visions we press into in prayer: a nation fully engulfed with the fire of God's presence. Allow the Lord to fill your thoughts with what it would look like if hundreds of thousands, even millions, of Canadians came to Christ.

The joy would be ubiquitous, and testimonies of what God was doing would even break into the evening news. Spontaneous worship, like an unorchestrated flash mob, would fill city subway cars and bustling downtown streets. University classes would be taken over with testifying and spontaneous preaching, while His presence would be tangible everywhere.....

It's not just sanctified daydreaming, but we are called to lift our eyes to see the ripeness and beauty of the harvest, to catch the vision of it's magnitude and the joy its ingathering will bring (John 4:35). Allow your heart to dream, allow your faith to rise. Like God said to Abraham: "Come outside the tent, and look up—look at the stars."

There is more, much more. Whatever has been attained, in spiritual breakthrough, harvest, and encounter with God as a spiritual high watermark, is not only attainable again, but there is more for us now. We don't look back at the golden "glory days" of when God was moving in past generations with nostalgia and longing, but we look ahead for the greatest move of God our nation (or your nation) has ever seen. The best is yet to come. We don't just say this as an encouraging, "keep-your-chin-up" pep talk. We say it because it is the nature of the kingdom of God to continually increase (Is 9:7, Dn 2:44, Mt 13:32, 11:12), and because Jesus is soon returning for a bride that is ready.

All over the nation (and every nation), across every denomination and all through the generations, the most prayed prayer has been the centrepiece of the Lord's Prayer: "Come, kingdom of God, be done, will of God—on earth as it is in heaven." Millions pray this daily; it's how Jesus instructed us to pray, a prayer that reveals His heartbeat for lives and our nation. With this cumulative, unrelenting intercession, how can we imagine that the kingdom of God has passed its prime, or that it wouldn't break in with even greater power, impact, and glory than ever before? It surely will.

Most certainly, the greatest, most stunning days of revival are immediately before us.

So What Brings Revival?

What brings revival is a perpetual question that the Church asks and answers in different ways, depending on our theological persuasion and our experience. What brings revival? Is revival our sovereign God, choosing in His wisdom and divine plan, to move intensely upon a place and a people, with the first thing He does to awaken prayer, faith, and hunger?

Or is it, as others would say, a divine response to persistent cries filled with faith and desire? Essentially this comes down to: Does it begin with us or with God?

In my younger days, as I studied historic revivals and sat under the preaching of Leonard Ravenhill, Winkie Pratney, and others, I was fully convinced the responsibility lay with the Church to "pray in" revival.

But after decades and hopefully deepening a bit in my theology, I've come to a bit of a hybrid position, so if you were to ask me if God moves in revival by His own sovereign will or in response to the prayers and hunger of His people, I'd say yes. I believe it's both.

"If my people who are called by my name humble themselves and pray and seek my face and turn from their wicked ways, then I will hear from heaven and will forgive their sin and heal their land." 2 Chronicles 7:14 ESV

God releases waves of His Spirit to revive the Church like great contractions in each generation, providing us with glorious opportunities for encounters with Him. As He does this, He awakens a deep hunger in the hearts of those He's planning to use, giving them grace for prayer and uncommon passion for the lost.

He's Delighted to be Interrupted

That being said, He also is quite willing and even delighted to be interrupted by brave, even obnoxious, faith. Think of how Jesus walked when on earth (remembering Jesus is the prefect representation of the Father). There were times when He had a definite plan to release His power—for example, when He went to Bethany to raise Lazarus (Jn 11:11) or when He sent His disciples to Bethsaida and followed them walking on water (Mk 6:45).

But there were other times when He was interrupted by someone being lowered through the roof, a blind man named Bartimaeus refusing to be quiet or a timid lady, desperately sick, grabbing the outer edge of His robe with faith. He's always willing to be sidetracked or "delayed" when faith puts caution aside, seizes the moment, and connects with His heart.

He even coaches us to be brave and obnoxious (in a totally sanctified kind of way) when He taught us the parable of the neighbor who needed bread.

"Then Jesus said to them, 'Suppose you have a friend, and you go to him at midnight and say, "Friend, lend me three loaves of bread; a friend of mine on a journey has come to me, and I have no food to offer him."

"'And suppose the one inside answers, "Don't bother me. The door is already locked, and my children and I are in bed. I can't get up and give you anything." I tell you, even though he will not get up and give you the bread because of friendship, yet because of your shameless audacity, he will surely get up and give you as much as you need.'"
Luke 11:5–8 NIV

So for me, this means the full responsibility to "pray in" revival doesn't rest on my shoulders (hallelujah), but the opportunity is open for me to shamelessly and audaciously contend for the glory of heaven to come crashing into my nation. It's up to me to relentlessly pursue Him with a heart on fire for His presence. It's been these ones—these that will give themselves to seriously go after revival—historically and scripturally that God is more than willing to respond to. It's both and. He comes to us of His own accord, and if we pursue Him, He loves it all the more.

"Call to me and I will answer you, and will tell you great and hidden things that you have not known." Jeremiah 33:3

"The Lord is near to all who call on him, to all who call on him in truth." Psalms 145:18

"If you then, though you are evil, know how to give good gifts to your children, how much more will your Father in heaven give the Holy Spirit to those who ask him!" Luke 11:13

Our Stories

Anything God has ever done, He can do now.

Anything God has ever done anywhere, He can do here.

Anything God has ever done for anyone,

He can do for you.

A.W. Tozer

Chapter 2

Henry Alline–The New Light Revival

An American who immigrated to Nova Scotia as a young child with his strict Puritan parents, Henry Alline lived and ministered in Canada during the years of the Great Awakening in New England.

It was the 1700s, long before Canadian confederation, before the railway, before the vision of Canada being more than a colony of either France or England had even been conceived. These were days of pioneering. Halifax had just been founded in this raw and hostile land. France and England's armies were still contending for the upper hand in the colonies, and the Battle of the Plains of Abraham was about to be fought.

There was little that made ministry easy—a sparse, spread-out population, telegrams, electricity and penicillin had yet to be invented. Roads were unpaved; life was simple and rough. Yet God was as present and actively drawing the hearts of the early pioneers and settlers of Canada as He is today.

Through his childhood and youth, Henry Alline hungered for God but struggled with tremendous internal spiritual conflict. It was the norm in those days to view God as an angry, distant, and judgmental old man ready to punish those who transgressed His laws. While Alline had been well schooled through his childhood in the Scriptures and theology, there was no clear revelation of God's love to awaken his heart. In these years, for the vast majority, Christianity had been reduced to an intellectual belief, devoid of any actual spiritual life or relationship with the Lord. Life was expected to be about doing your duty and maintaining outward righteousness, without the inward reality or of empowerment of God's presence or love.

So although there was a deep drawing to the Lord, what Alline had tasted of Christianity did nothing to address his spiritual hunger.

Yet in spite of all the darkness and coldness around him, at age twenty-seven, Alline was powerfully converted through an intense encounter with the love of God. He records in his journal, "Redeeming love broke into my soul with repeated scriptures with such power that my whole soul seemed melted down with love."[2] Everything changed; he was a man on fire. A year later, in 1778, even without formal theological training, he yielded to the call he believed God put on his life and stepped into the ministry, travelling by horseback as an itinerant preacher, through the Maritime provinces of Nova Scotia, New Brunswick, Prince Edward Island, and into the New England states of America.[3]

The revelation he carried of God's love and the reality of heaven and hell overflowed into his preaching. It was a new and welcome sound; it touched the hearts and awakened revival.

Alline became know as the "Whitfield of Nova Scotia" as he adopted the fiery preaching style of the New Light revivalists, a movement of the Great Awakening primarily led by George Whitfield. Alline's powerful preaching shook the region, challenging the dead religious form and unconverted ministers in the Church. His gospel repeatedly appealed to the hearts of the Maritimers and called for personal conversions, rather than just an intellectual alignment with the doctrines of Christianity; it was passionate, fiery, and fruitful. But he became strongly opposed by the religious elite, whom he challenged, and numerous ministers rose up to thwart him.

Here is another excerpt from his journal: "O the damage that is done by unconverted ministers, and legal professors. I have found them in my travels more inveterate [resistant] against the power of religion than the openly profane. But blessed be God, although they left no stone unturned to obstruct what they call a delusion; yet the work still increases."[4]

The ministers of the gospel were appalled by Alline's assertions that they, and many of their congregants, were not actually saved and needed to be thoroughly converted. He preached that they were "the blind leading the blind." Understandably, invitations welcoming him to the region's pulpits became harder and harder to find.

Shut Out of the Church

So as invitations to preach dried up as a result of his refusal to compromise, Alline gathered crowds in barns or open fields, relentless in his preaching and travel. His journal records the intensity of his labours for the gospel and the zeal of the Lord that burned in his heart.

"Rode thirty miles and although I was so fatigued by riding in heavy rain that I could scarcely walk when I got from my horse, yet when I began to preach, I had such a sense of the redeemer's cause, that I almost forgot my bodily infirmities.

"I preached so often and rode so much that sometimes I would seem almost worn out and yet in a few hours would be so refreshed that I could labor again for twelve hours in discoursing, praying, preaching, and exhorting and feel strong in my lungs."[5]

Awakened the Maritimes

In his wake, eight New Light churches were planted and five hundred hymns penned, but his legacy is much more extensive than these outward signs. Many say all of Nova Scotia and New Brunswick, as well as parts of PEI and even New England, was awakened through his short, intense ministry.[6] The revival he birthed became the sure foundation for the Baptist movement in the Maritimes, which remains today a vibrant contributor to the spiritual life of these provinces.

Alline's zeal and passion for souls drove himself incessantly until he succumbed to tuberculosis after only seven years of ministry. His tombstone holds this epitaph: "Henry Alline, 1748–1784, died at the age of 35. Like a flame of fire, he swept through the land. He was a burning and shining light. After zealous travels in the cause of Christ, he languished on the way and cheerfully resigned his life. He was vastly esteemed as the Apostle of Nova Scotia."[7]

On the Name of Jesus

by Henry Alline

Jesus we love thy Name
And thee we will adore
And when we feel this Heavenly flame
We long to Love Thee more.

Thy Name is all our trust
Thy Name is Solid peace
Thy Name is everlasting rest
When other Names shall Cease.

There Ravish'd with thy Name
We nevermore shall rove
There sound thine everlasting fame
And Solace in thy Love.

Thy Name shall be our Praise
Thy Name shall be our Joy
Thy Name thro Everlasting Days
Shall Countless throngs Employ.[8]

Chapter 3

The Call to Zeal

"Never be lacking in zeal, but keep your
spiritual fervor, serving the Lord."
–Romans 12:11 NIV

The more we insert ourselves into the life and times of Henry Alline and seek to understand the pressures and opposition he faced, the more inspiring, even challenging, his story is. To preach relentlessly, at great personal cost, a message that cut a completely different path from the established ministers of the Church took boldness and conviction. To continue on after being shut out of their pulpits, mocked and dismissed as fanatical by those he had been raised to respect, took a true gift of fire. As perhaps Canada's first revivalist, for Alline to be compared to John the Baptist seems entirely appropriate. He certainly was a voice consumed with the love of God, crying in the wilderness.

"The voice of one crying in the wilderness:
'Prepare the way of the Lord,
make his paths straight,'"
John appeared, baptizing in the wilderness and proclaiming a baptism
of repentance for the forgiveness of sins." Mark 1:3,4

"He was a burning and shining lamp, and you were willing to rejoice
for a while in his light." John 5:35

It seems Henry Alline couldn't have stayed silent, even if he tried. His life was overflowing with the revelation of God's love, the dark eternity before the unsaved, and the zeal of the Lord. Like John the Baptist, he was a "burning and shining lamp" and was aflame with fasting, prayer, and a spirit of revival. He was a man commissioned by the Lord to preach and proclaim the truth of the gospel, but it was zeal that made him so extraordinarily fruitful.

Even though zeal today is often considered a sign of immaturity, or lack of balance, yet Jesus himself was a man of zeal when He walked the earth.

"His disciples remembered that it was written, 'Zeal for your house will consume me'." John 2:17

Wisdom Leads to Zeal

More often well-meaning friends will caution us to pursue balance in our lives, rather than embracing in the zeal of God as Henry Alline did. In Scripture we see the first and greatest commandment is to love God. Not to love Him in a measured, balanced, cautious way but to love Him full throttle, with everything we have—heart, soul, mind, and strength. Loving Him with nothing held back or in reserve, but with all the fire and passion, zeal and abandonment we can give. This is how Jesus demonstrated His love for us on the cross; there was nothing "balanced" about it. He was "all in," and He still is.

The pursuit of balance is actually a Buddhist value; it's trying to find that perfect tension between opposing sides. But Scripture instructs us to walk in wisdom rather than balance, and wisdom always involves love and obedience. Wisdom will protect us from foolish excess of work, spending, or being distracted with temporal pleasures, but while wisdom gives us principles to live by, obedience to the Spirit often calls us to a higher priority of eternal values.

17

This is how Henry Alline lived: in fiery obedience. If he had cooled down and not worked himself so hard, would he have preserved his health and lived a longer life, potentially much more fruitful? It's possible, but it could also be that God was moving in a spirit of revival, and Alline seized the moment with everything he had, even if it cost him his health and eventually his life. When we look at the book of Acts, we see this is thoroughly scriptural. Could it have been that the zeal with which he pursued ministry was as much a message in itself about the love of God as his words? It was a voice of fire that was needed awaken people out of a dull, dead, intellectual faith—an awakening that couldn't have happened with a more measured approach.

The passion and zeal with which Alline lived was consistent with the message of the wonder of God's love and the urgency of the condition of sinners. It would not have landed with such an impact if it had come from a man walking out his faith in a casual way; the contradiction of life and message would have stripped his preaching of its convicting power.

Our National Sin

It has been said of Canada that our national sin is apathy. Internationally we are known as people with a high value on peace, on polite, respectful society, and on apologizing for anything and everything (even if we are not at fault). You know you are in Canada when you accidentally run into someone with your grocery cart and they turn around and apologize! But even though this value of our culture is used of God in a redemptive way, as He anoints the church in the nation for being powerfully used in healing, reconciliation, and peace, it has a downside as well. The "flesh" side of this peaceful culture is being resistant to passion, to scorn zeal as excessive and unbalanced.

Apathy, if we let it, muzzles the fire of love and passion for Jesus, the cry for souls, and the lifestyle of sacrifice and pursuit. Apathy looks upon an alabaster jar that's being smashed to pour love on Jesus and pulls back in quiet, critical judgments. It's a heavy, wet blanket of indifference that places our comfort, convenience, and ease as an idol we value above all else. It's so pervasive and at times intense that we must live in a place were we intentionally and continually choose fervency, pushing back the encroaching dullness and spiritual slumber.

But if we desire the mantle of zeal our forefather carried in this land as an inheritance that's stored up for us by what he pioneered, we can have it!

The Zeal of the Lord Consumes Christ

Henry Alline modeled it here in Canada, but Jesus, the One who carries all the fire and desire of heaven, lives within us if we are believers. He is the one who was driven to prayer, out of the depth of His desire for His bride, again and again, as He walked on earth. He was the one who carried the cross and laid His holy life upon it. He went all the way for us. He is now the one who continues in this ministry of intercession, seated at the right hand of the Father. His eyes burn with fire; the zeal of the Lord continues to consume Him.

We can access His passion; we can enter into agreement with His fiery desire for the whole nation to be saved, both those that have never heard of His great love, and those that have willfully and continually rejected it. His heart has not cooled toward those that once walked with Him but have journeyed far down the prodigal road. He wants them all. He paid for them all. Touching the zeal for souls in the heart of Christ is something that has marked revivalists all through history.

He's also passionate for the Church. How Jesus loves His bride and longs for her to be mature, spotless, and complete. He sees how our immaturity hurts us and hurts each other. He is well aware of the mixture of truth and error that brings confusion and dysfunction. He sees into our hearts and understands when we wrestle and succumb to sinful, fleshly desires, even while He's pouring out His grace to strengthen us in our time of need. Jesus loves the Church, and His great desire for her to be clothed in the spotless, wrinkle-free wedding dress is more for our sake than for His. Our sin, weakness, and immaturity hurt us and hinders us so deeply.

There is also a vision and passion in the heart of God for our nation to fulfill our end-time destiny and for this land to be an explosive launching pad for the global missions movement. We haven't been given a well-educated, skilled nation rich in resources but also extraordinarily multicultural so that we could all live very pleasant lives. No, Canada is called to the nations, and one of the most wonderful fruits of revival is when, on the heels of a move of God, the mission movement explodes with hundreds of new volunteers.

Living in Zeal

Living in a place of zeal requires that we are alert to the coldness and spiritual indifference in the atmosphere, like a strong headwind, and compensate with walking in the opposite spirit to stay on course with the heart of Jesus. But it's not something we can do in the flesh.

Zeal that is hyped up—where emotions are stirred or where there is a rallying call to be fervent yet no root system of intimacy with Jesus, no revelation of His heart, no gazing upon His matchless worth—will not last. It ends in burnout and disillusionment. Maintaining a walk of zeal requires the power of the Spirit and the fire of love. Duty isn't strong enough to withstand this prevailing headwind; performance can't sustain you in the secret place when no one is watching. The fire must come from love.

"Set me as a seal upon your heart, as a seal upon your arm, for love is strong as death; jealousy is fierce as the grave. Its flashes are flashes of fire, the very flame of the Lord. Many waters cannot quench love, neither can floods drown it. If a man offered for love all the wealth of his house, he would be utterly despised." Song of Solomon 8:6,7 ESV

Praying with Zeal

As we lead prayer in Redleaf, we have to continually pursue this place of zeal. It's not about loud, dramatic prayer, although our emotions should be engaged as we go after God; yet we can't get there by performance. Fervent prayer involves repeatedly, daily, connecting with God's heart for a need or an issue and allowing our passion to get invested. We must choose to involve our hearts and care deeply about that which we are praying for, because it's what profoundly matters to Him. Somehow, in the mystery of God, when we invest ourselves in this way, prayer genuinely becomes a mighty force that shakes nations.

"The effective, fervent prayer of a righteous man avails much." James 5:16b NKJV

The zeal that possessed Henry Alline's life came from his intense encounter with the raw love of God. He was undone and transformed forever with the revelation of Jesus's heart. It sustained him on the path of zeal through opposition of every kind, including every physical ordeal, illness, and hardship.

That zeal is as available for us as it was for Alline. If we will ask, and keep on asking, God will give us our own moments of encounter with His passion. He will sustain us in the intimacy that will overflow into a life marked by zeal so that a whole new company of "burning and shining lamps" will arise in the land.

Chapter 4

The Hamilton Revival–1857

Revival historians have credited this three-year revival as the initial spark that began the Third Great Awakening, which then blazed across much of the globe in the mid-1800s! It was a spark that began in Hamilton, a community of twenty-three thousand people, just west of Toronto.

The lay preaching team of Walter and Phoebe Palmer from New York City began ministering in Canada through a camp meeting in 1853, which was held at a farm near Nappanee, Ontario. They were overjoyed with the strong response as five hundred people gave their lives to Christ. The following year, they returned to Nappanee, and Church historian Gerald Procee recorded what Walter penned to his daughters: "The meetings I cannot describe to you; there were hundreds converted. It was one of the most glorious meetings I ever attended."[9]

Two years later, in 1855, the Palmers returned to hold meetings in Barrie, and again, hundreds found Christ. While these salvations were wonderful breakthroughs, the region was being prepared for an even greater move of God.

Hamilton and the surrounding area was a major stronghold of Methodism, which in the 1850s was a vibrant, passionate expression of Christianity, given to the pursuit of revival. Fervent prayer and preaching with intense calls to repentance and consecration were a part of the Methodist experience. The Grimsby campground, not too far from Hamilton, was especially used of God, as annually, high profile, anointed preachers would minister to campers during the summer.

In October of 1857, the Palmers had again been ministering in Canada and were on their way back to New York after doing a series of successful evangelistic meetings. Their luggage had been lost, however, so they decided to stay with friends in Hamilton longer than originally expected as they waited for their luggage to be retrieved.

A wise, local Methodist minister discovered they were in town and seized the opportunity. Gathering the three downtown Methodist churches, he hosted a joint prayer meeting on the Thursday, with about sixty-five in attendance.

Phoebe Palmer, the firebrand evangelist, spoke, challenging the saints to commit themselves to serious prayer for revival. Gerald Procee gives an account: "About sixty-five persons were in attendance, and they were challenged to pray for revival. Some thirty of them raised their hands, indicating that they would earnestly give themselves to engage in prayer for revival. They would not only engage in personal, fervent prayer but also seek to take fellow Hamiltonians with them to church."[10]

Clearly God was ordaining the circumstances, and the Palmers could sense that an "effectual door of ministry" had opened for them and the kingdom. They eagerly responded with a willingness to hold a series of impromptu meetings in the pursuit of revival.

Prayer Bears Immediate Fruit

The next day during the first united revival meeting, Phoebe again preached with power, and immediately twenty-one responded to the salvation appeal. At the close of the Saturday meeting, another twenty rushed to the altar, and on Sunday the number climbed to seventy-five.[11] The following week, meetings were held from seven in the morning until ten at night. These were times of the glorious presence of God—deep encounters, repentance, and hearts laid bare before the Lord. As a result they also overflowed with testimonies of His power and grace.

After ten days of meetings, four hundred had been won into the kingdom, and the revival was stirring through the city, particularly in Methodist circles. Sadly, however, some of the other denominations lived through these times virtually unaware of what was happening in their midst.

The newspapers even reported on the revival, and *The Christian Guardian* on October 28, 1857, blazed with the headline: "*A Revival After Apostolic Times.*" The article went on to report: "We are happy to report to our lovers of Zion [Methodist Church], that a most glorious revival is now going on in Hamilton."

The Mayor Comes to Christ

The Christian Advocate, from New York City, also reported of the revival on November 5, 1857: "The work is taking with its range... persons of all classes. Men from a low degree and men of high estate for wealth and position, all men and maidens, and even little children are seen humbly kneeling together, pleading for grace. The Mayor of the city with other persons of like position is not ashamed to be seen bowed at the altar of prayer beside their humble servant."[12]

In fact the mayor, John Moore, was one of the ones most deeply touched by the power of God as the Lord poured out revival on the city.

The extended meetings lasted well into November, by which time over a thousand had been saved,[13] and the city fully awakened. The Palmers returned to New York, but the work continued, sustained by passionate prayer and the power of testimony.

The revival's impact on the Methodist community was extraordinary. Daina Doucet, in the article she wrote about the revival for *The Beacon* in July of 2007, reports that the churches grew in attendance by a thousand percent. These weren't just casual pew-warmers. These newly born-again

Methodists had been plunged into the power of the Spirit and were being used of God. Phoebe Palmer, continued with a month long campaign and regularly preached on sanctification accompanied by an invitation to receive the fullness of the Spirit, which she called the "baptism of fire."[14]

Uniquely, these were also Christians, saved into a move of God that was led by lay ministers rather than professional clergy, so everyone became aware that prayer and proclamation was something they all could participate in and in fact had been commissioned to do so. This was a revolutionary concept. Because of this, an army of revivalists arose.

Layman's Revival Trigered

New York, soon after, also experienced the same spirit that was released in Hamilton when the Laymen's Revival erupted out of the noon-hour Fulton Street prayer meetings. In seven months ninety-six thousand new believers had encountered Christ.

Was it the Hamilton revival that triggered what became known as the Third Great Awakening? Revival historians, such as Richard Riss of New Jersey, believe it was and trace the initial spark of the prayer-birthed move of the Spirit, the Layman's Revival, to Hamilton.[15]

We know that revivals are highly contagious. When there is desire, hunger, or need, a revival will spread. If God is moving nearby, it's very common for the revival to spark faith, and if mixed with persistent prayer in another region or town, the result is the same type of the movement of the Spirit or even greater.

Perhaps Hamilton was the trigger or perhaps the move of God in Hamilton and New York simply both broke out independently based on each city's longing for God, commitment to prayer, and willingness to humble themselves. Either way, we are profoundly thankful for the glorious legacy of the revival fire that erupted and circled the globe as the Third Great Awakening took the nations by storm. We are thankful Canada was touched by this fire.

Chapter 5

Humility Draws the Spirit

"For thus says the One who is high and lifted up, who inhabits eternity, whose name is Holy: "I dwell in the high and holy place, and also with him who is of a contrite and lowly spirit, to revive the spirit of the lowly, and to revive the heart of the contrite."
— Isaiah 57:15

While the church in Hamilton is highly aware of the history of the Phoebe Palmer Revival, generally, the rest of the nation isn't, and there is even less awareness beyond the borders of Canada. It's a wonderful story and a story that highlights how hunger, that is truly hunger, will receive from any vessel, and receive at any cost.

In 2 Kings, Naaman, the powerful commander, was desperate for healing from leprosy. In spite of his position and resources, this incurable disease made his situation extremely dire. Leprosy didn't just lead to a debilitated, shortened life, but it was particularly feared because of the isolation, rejection, and poverty that a leper lived in.

Naaman knew the only cure for this disease was a supernatural touch from God, so he pursued the prophet Elijah for his healing. But when the response from the prophet came, he was insulted. Dip seven times in the Jordan!? Surely there was a grander, more dignified way to receive from God, something more befitting his high stature in society. Naaman was on the verge of turning his miracle away out of pride when the servant girl intervened.

"Naaman, commander of the army of the king of Syria, was a great man with his master and in high favor, because by him the Lord had given victory to Syria. He was a mighty man of valor, but he was a leper. Now the Syrians on one of their raids had carried off a little girl from the land of Israel, and she worked in the service of Naaman's wife. She said to her mistress, "Would that my lord were with the prophet who is in Samaria! He would cure him of his leprosy." So Naaman went in and told his lord, "Thus and so spoke the girl from the land of Israel." And the king of Syria said, "Go now, and I will send a letter to the king of Israel."

So he went, taking with him ten talents of silver, six thousand shekels of gold, and ten changes of clothing. And he brought the letter to the king of Israel, which read, "When this letter reaches you, know that I have sent to you Naaman my servant, that you may cure him of his leprosy." And when the king of Israel read the letter, he tore his clothes and said, "Am I God, to kill and to make alive, that this man sends word to me to cure a man of his leprosy? Only consider, and see how he is seeking a quarrel with me."

But when Elisha, the man of God, heard that the king of Israel had torn his clothes, he sent to the king, saying, "'Why have you torn your clothes? Let him come now to me, that he may know that there is a prophet in Israel."

So Naaman came with his horses and chariots and stood at the door of Elisha's house. And Elisha sent a messenger to him, saying, "Go and wash in the Jordan seven times, and your flesh shall be restored, and you shall be clean." But Naaman was angry and went away, saying, "Behold, I thought that he would surely come out to me and stand and call upon the name of the Lord his God, and wave his hand over the place and cure the leper. Are not Abana and Pharpar, the rivers of Damascus, better than all the waters of Israel? Could I not wash in them and be clean". So he turned and went away in a rage.

But his servants came near and said to him, "My father, it is a great word the prophet has spoken to you; will you not do it? Has he actually said to you, 'Wash, and be clean'?" So he went down and dipped himself seven times in the Jordan, according to the word of the man of God, and his flesh was restored like the flesh of a little child, and he was clean." 2 Kings 5:1–14

Humility is Always a Feature of Revival

Humility is always a feature of genuine revival, for God resists the proud and gives grace to the humble (Jas 4:6), and revival is most certainly a work of great grace. When we value our image and dignity more than the breakthrough and encounter with God that we need, our cold, hard hearts turn away opportunities for grace, and we resist conviction that leads us to the repentance that opens to door for revival. Pride cannot receive revival. We can save face or lose it at the foot of the cross, but O what a worthy exchange that is!

In the Victorian times of 1857, it was extremely rare for a woman to stand in a pulpit and to be received as a preacher. Women were considered intellectually inferior, emotional, and unreliable, so it took tremendous hunger, even humility, for men to gather under the preaching of a woman. But these men didn't go to see a curiosity; they went with hunger. They listened and, yielding to the power of the Spirit, responded wholeheartedly, coming to Christ in droves.

How this response of humility must have blessed the Father! Certainly heaven came down and kissed earth with a citywide awakening as the uncommon vessel of a woman became the messenger of grace. But it wasn't just the fact that Hamilton received the preaching of a woman, but humility became a particular mark of this revival as the altars filled with men and women of all social classes, shoulder to shoulder, equally in conviction and need of a Saviour.

Pride Pushes God Away

Pride is in the heart of all of us and needs to constantly be yielded to the work of the cross. Humility renders us soft and malleable for the Spirit to teach us, lead us, and use us. But pride always seeks to maintain self-respect and dignity; it's like that cat when dropped from any position quickly twists its body to land on its feet. Pride always lands on its feet; it always saves face.

But pride also pushes God and His grace away. God resists the proud because the proud resist Him in stubborn self and independence. If we pursue a life full of humility, God will use us and even entrust us with great honour. Humility will guard us from position, power or prestige inflating our self-image, and enables us to continue in dependence and giving Him the glory even when highly honoured.

Authentic humility is needed to go to a deep place of repentance. Pride, seeking to land on its feet and save as much face as possible, will justify or minimize sin. It will offload blame and transfer it to our parents or a spouse or others at hand. This is where church leadership often gets blamed, as we excuse our responsibility for our own sin, and our own heart's condition. There is always self-justification, defensiveness, and deflecting in a proud heart. It's like the parable of the sinner and the Pharisee. The Pharisee proudly assumed he was righteous, while the tax collector, though on the outside, more obviously sinful, owned his sin and fully acknowledged his need of mercy. And mercy he was granted.

"He also told this parable to some who trusted in themselves that they were righteous, and treated others with contempt: "Two men went up into the temple to pray, one a Pharisee and the other a tax collector. The Pharisee, standing by himself, prayed thus: 'God, I thank you that I am not like other men, extortioners, unjust, adulterers, or even like this tax collector. I fast twice a week; I give tithes of all that I get.'

But the tax collector, standing far off, would not even lift up his eyes to heaven, but beat his breast, saying, 'God, be merciful to me, a sinner!

I tell you, this man went down to his house justified, rather than the other. For everyone who exalts himself will be humbled, but the one who humbles himself will be exalted." Luke 18:9–14

What is Humility?

So what then is humility? It's not outward display of groveling, running ourselves down, or rebuffing compliments or affirmations. It's not refusing to be acknowledged for our contributions or abilities, but it is recognizing that we are not the source. Bill Gothard, the respected Bible teacher, defines it like this: "Humility is recognizing that it is God and others who are responsible for the achievements in my life."

Fred Smith, writing in *Christianity Today Journal of Leadership* says: "Humility is not denying the power you have but admitting the power comes through you, not from you."[16] It's not denying that we have any worth or any skills but recognizing we didn't achieve them alone.

Humility doesn't deny what God has done in our lives or diminish the role we play in the kingdom, but it simply doesn't take primary credit for the victories or achievements. It won't take the credit, or the glory, no matter how hard you insist.

When you are with people of humility, it's wonderfully refreshing. They are comfortable stepping up to lead or sitting in the back row cheering others on. They are fulfilled and content in either place, never needing the spotlight or refusing to step up and contribute for fear of making a mistake and embarrassing themselves. A humble person can be praised and stay grounded without his or her ego being pumped up. They continually choose to live without a facade, which makes them approachable and a safe, nonjudgmental place for the openness and transparency of others. This is certainly a virtue we all need more of.

Creating Atmospheric Change

A powerful feature of humility is its capacity to suddenly create such a glorious, spiritual atmosphere change. When humility is authentically modeled, it challenges and inspires others to follow suit, even when that was not at all the intention. It doesn't take much to release the fragrance of humility, and once released, it is irresistible. Even hardened, cynical, secular society loves and respects the fragrance of humility; it's looked at as a strength and mark of true character. How much more is humility attractive to heaven, for it's so Christlike!

A pastor friend of mine recently illustrated this in a beautiful way. He has a successful ministry, a vibrant church and is frequently called to minister internationally. Yet his primary mandate is to pastor his people. The Holy Spirit had been bringing conviction to his heart, concerning his need to invest more intentionally in his church and the key leadership relationships, rather than ministering externally.

He didn't seek to spin it, save face, or subtly shift the blame to others, but he stood in front of his whole church during the Sunday service and, with tears of repentance, confessed he had gotten distracted and off track and was now setting this right. He wasn't performing or seeking to model something; he was confessing sin, with a broken and contrite heart, and asking for forgiveness. You can imagine the response to this humility; the fragrance of it filled the room, and like electricity the presence of God rushed in. Rather than his congregation lowering their respect for him and trust in his leadership, it went through the roof!

Humility Makes Us Teachable

When we live in humility, not only do we concern ourselves more with what God thinks than saving face, but we are also genuinely teachable and can receive from even the most unlikely, untaught, inexperienced vessels. We see what God has put in them—how the Lord has gifted them to contribute to the body of Christ, even if they seem to be a "Jordan River." It's not

31

about patronizing each other with flattery and false honour; it's having eyes to genuinely see great value and be able to learn from anyone.

Jesus, the creator of the universe, humbled Himself more than we can even conceive as He took on human form, not just any human but a baby (presumed illegitimate) birthed into a poor family in an occupied land. As the oldest child in the family, Jesus suffered through novice parents and graciously submitted, was taught, and guided as He grew. Such a glorious example of humility! If Christ, the King of Glory, can submit in this way, surely we should all the more.

Pastor Bob Birch also modeled this so well. I'll never forget the time when Mike and I were helping lead a house church after the Lord had led us out of St. Margaret's. Pastor Bob and his wife, Margaret, used to attend whenever they were able, enjoying the freshness and hunger of this wineskin. We were all in our thirties at this point, and the Birches were well into their sixties (at least), with decades of experience in ministry and national stature, as well as deep anointing in revival. Yet they never took over or came with a patronizing attitude; in fact Pastor Bob would earnestly ask, "What is God saying to you?" with a full expectation that each of us would have revelation and insight into the heart of God that he didn't.

Consider these verses from one of Pastor Bob's favourite chapters of scripture:

"I am the vine; you are the branches. Whoever abides in me and I in him, he it is that bears much fruit, for apart from me you can do nothing." John 15:5

What a joy to have been in the crowd that day that Phoebe Palmer spoke and Hamilton responded in hunger and humility! We can only imagine how beautiful and intense the presence of God must have been as He poured out His Spirit on the city in response to these tender hearts. But even in this day, this humility is accessible to all of us; it's biblically a command, an invitation, and a choice.

Chapter 6

Hunter and Crossley–1888

John Hunter and Hugh Crossley were Methodist ministers that God yoked together to form a dynamic revival team to shake their generation. Because of the anointing and fruitfulness of their partnership, they were commissioned to travel and conduct evangelistic revival meetings throughout Ontario with phenomenal results.

John Hunter was saved at age fifteen into the Methodist revival culture. He was wholehearted and zealous from the very beginning of his life in Christ; it was as if he had been created to love God and preach the gospel. He was on fire! Passion for souls and winning them into the kingdom came easily and naturally.

He entered Victoria College in Cobourg, Ontario, and here his evangelistic gift was nurtured and honed. It wasn't just instruction he received, however. It was also the work of the Spirit in his life, as the Lord prepared his heart to carry the message of the gospel with intense fire. Here also John Hunter and Hugh Crossley met, and they spurred each other on in their zealous pursuit of the Lord.

Their ministry partnership began with holding revival meetings for the students of Victoria College, sparking a move of God right on the campus. It was like a sign of first fruits, an indication of the massive harvest that they would to see come into the kingdom through their shared commitment to preaching the gospel and seeing souls saved.

As they launched into formal ministry, they were an immediate success; in their first year twenty-five hundred commitments to Christ were made. They were invited to Toronto to conduct meetings for a month, and ended up with fifty-five meetings addressing between seventy-five thousand and one hundred thousand people. They did not just preach salvation without the lordship of Christ but spoke at length about a life of holiness and the need to live out faith in every area of one's life.

The team of Crossley and Hunter was credited with leading over two hundred thousand people to publicly give their lives to Christ over the span of their ministry. They were called the greatest evangelists of their generation. *Toronto Daily Mail and Empire*'s published obituary for Hugh Crossley reads: "The late Mr. Crossley brought more converts to the penitent's form than any other single individual of his generation."[17] Under their ministry, the spiritual character of many Ontario towns changed visibly. Pubs and bars were frequently emptied, and on several occasions theatres closed for lack of business.

Awakening in Ottawa

But with all their success and fruit, the most significant time was the move of God that awakened Ottawa in the winter of 1888.

Crossley and Hunter had been holding a six-week series of meetings, and several senators, members of parliament, and even the Prime Minister, Sir John A. MacDonald, had been attending. At the final night of the planned meetings, after the searching sermon by John Hunter, he gave an appeal for anyone who wished to become Christians. Canada's Prime Minister and his wife rose to their feet, and the newspaper of the day reported "many strong men bowed their heads and wept for joy. The right honorable gentleman himself was deeply affected."[18] After dining at the Prime Minister's home several days later, Hunter confirmed: "Sir John is a changed man."[19]

The call to Christ that the Prime Minister yielded to was also a call to righteousness and reforming Canada with biblical values. It wasn't meant to be a private faith, but a faith that brought the convictions of righteousness to bear in the public arena. Mayors, senators, and members of parliament also joined MacDonald in his newfound desire to see Canada become a land that truly reflected the call of Psalms 72:8, that had influenced its name: the Dominion of Canada.

"May he have dominion from sea to sea, and from the River to the ends of the earth!"[20]

Chapter 7

Anointed Preaching

"Preach the word...do the work of
an evangelist."
—1 Timothy 4:2 & 5

The story of Crossley and Hunter is one that those who have a deep commitment to pray for government understandably cherish. Imagine the victory and breakthrough, as the first prime minister of our nation—widely known as a drunk—yields to the conviction of the Spirit of God and gives his life to Christ in a public setting. This is certainly a "do-it-again" moment that we can ask for in prayer and not for just for our prime minister, but for all the influencers in the elite of government, media, business and education. Truly anyone can be touched and drawn to the cross, but especially in a time of awakening and revival.

But what moved the heart of the prime minister, and the hundreds of thousands who also were saved under the ministry of Crossley and Hunter, was the anointing on their preaching. These weren't just sermons crafted with persuasive words and rational arguments; neither were they men simply skilled in manipulating emotions, but they walked in an anointing that awakened slumbering souls to their need of a Saviour and brought to them the urgency of the moment.

How does revival anointing empower preaching to bring forth this level of kingdom fruit? What makes it different than the good solid preaching used by God weekly basis to edify and strengthen the Church? These are certainly questions for which the Church has long sought to find definitive answers. The answers we like, however, are the simple how-tos and "six easy steps to revival preaching." But God will never be reduced to formulas and templates that we can follow that don't require an intimate relationship with Him.

The whole idea of revival is God coming near, and relationship with Him exploding throughout a community, not us using Him as merely a means to get the Church into a more successful or happier place. We have to always go back to the heartbeat of Christianity: God dwelling with man. But to get there, He has given us principles, which He values, and He reveals them in His word.

Let's look at the first revival sermon in the book of Acts on the day of Pentecost. Here, revival preaching shines, and there are a few things that become apparent.

A Focus on Christ

On the backdrop of the outpouring of the Holy Spirit, Peter stands with the other apostles and begins to speak (Acts 2:14). He proclaims over the confusion and clamour the revelation of what was happening in their midst. He sets the focus squarely on Jesus and begins to demonstrate that Jesus is God, that He is the son of David and Messiah.

Scriptures roll off of Peter's tongue as the Spirit quickens him and inspires him. Every argument is silenced as this unschooled fisherman exalts Jesus and powerfully convinces the multitude that the supernatural sign they were all witnessing was an endorsement from heaven of the Lordship of Christ.

All through the Scriptures, as theophanies occur, the response is consistent—a overwhelming awareness of the stark difference between the holiness of God and our lives, which is so often filled with mixture, compromise, and the spirit of the world.

So it is with anointed preaching. It reveals Christ, and suddenly as we are aware of the gap between who He is and how we live, we respond with "Woe is me, I am a man of unclean lips…"[21] Yet simultaneously, in a revival climate, God actively reveals the greatness of His love, and it utterly undoes, heals, restores and renews hearts. Anointed preaching reveals Christ.

Proclaiming the Truth

The brutal crucifixion of Jesus was still fresh in Peter's memory. He had shrunk back before when the threat of joining Jesus in his death presented itself, and his courage crumpled to the point where he denied he even knew Jesus.

But this Peter, restored by the Lord's tenderness and filled with the Spirit, was like a lion, boldly proclaiming not only who Christ was but that the Jews had rejected and crucified their long-awaited Messiah. Revival preaching has never minced words. While it's always revealed the love and mercy of God, it's equally exposed our desperate need of him.

Peter must have realized he was risking his life as he brought an accusation against the religious leaders for their involvement in Christ's death, yet still he did not hold back.

Peter proclaims to the religious leaders:

"This Jesus, delivered up according to the definite plan and foreknowledge of God, you crucified and killed by the hands of lawless men." Acts 2:23

In John, when Jesus taught of the coming of the Spirit He called Him initially the Spirit of Truth. This Spirit of Truth lands on and anoints truth (Jn14:16,17).

It's the work of the Spirit of Truth to convict the world of sin, righteousness, and judgment (Jn 16:8). But if our preaching is dancing

38

around the truth, so as not to offend anyone, or coming from a harsh religious condemnation rather than a Spirit-led, love-filled conviction, we won't see the results Peter did. Three thousand souls encountered Christ and were changed forever.

"Let all the house of Israel therefore know for certain that God has made him both Lord and Christ, this Jesus whom you crucified." Now when they heard this they were cut to the heart, and said to Peter and the rest of the apostles, "Brothers, what shall we do?" Acts 2:36,37

Today as we pray for revival many hours a day in the Red Leaf HOP, God so frequently draws our prayers to intercede for an uncompromised gospel, filled with the power of God, to be proclaimed from every pulpit in the nation. We need to pursue the anointing, not just to do signs and wonders (which is absolutely important) but to preach the truth of the gospel in a way that holy conviction grips hearts. It's then, with this conviction, that like the voice of the crowds before Peter or the jailer of Philippi in Paul's day, everyone cries out: "What must I do to be saved?!"

Conviction

I can't believe that conviction is old school, the experience of another age, irrelevant for this time. Because scriptural preaching ended in conviction, I can't believe that the message for today is all and only about God's love, goodness, and grace. Sin has always been what has separated us from God, and conviction is the glorious work of the Spirit that highlights our sin—not to shame us but to stir us to grab hold of the Saviour. It's what ignites repentance and sets our eyes upon the wonder of God's mercy poured out at the cross.

After Bible school in the late seventies, the Lord led me to a hotbed of passion for revival, just outside of a little town called Lindale in east Texas. It became a magnet for hungry young adults from across the United States, Canada, and even the British Commonwealth. Leaders like Winkie Pratney and Leonard Ravenhill lived right on the ministry campus teaching and mentoring these young zealots. Other leaders such as David Wilkerson, who trained his leaders next door, and Keith and Melody Green, who lived down the street, added their fire to the cluster of young revivalists in the area.

In that spiritual greenhouse, we were trained for ministry with the teachings of Charles Finney, William and Catherine Booth, CT Studd, Praying Hyde, and a whole range of other giants in faith who poured out their lives for the sake of revival, at home and on foreign fields. But one of the things I remember the most was what happened when Leonard Ravenhill preached.

The fear of the Lord would be so strong, the conviction of sin so acute, that I would tremble in the tangible presence of Holy God, praying earnestly King David's words, "search me and see if there be any wicked way in me" (Ps 139: 23,34). It wasn't that I didn't believe I was in Christ or that I had lost my confidence in His righteousness that clothed me, but I would be overwhelmed with the palpable Spirit of the Fear of the Lord that would rest upon Ravenhill's preaching (Is 11:2).

It is the goodness of God that leads men to repentance, but there are two ways to look at this verse[22] (which both reveal truth). It is a revelation of God's goodness that makes Him so attractive, in fact irresistible, so we repent for walking away from Him and run into His arms. When we preach in a way that pulls back the religious veil and reveals the goodness of God in this way, lives change. We absolutely need more of it; the gospel should always be good news!

But there is another way to look at this scripture, which takes the whole verse and context into account, not just the last phrase. It is that God, in His goodness, doesn't just allow a person to stumble into hell without striving to lead him or her to the point of repentance. This is the beauty of the cross. The incredible goodness of God reveals a man's sin, his or her need, and the path toward eternal hell that he or she is on and points the individual to the saving grace of Jesus.

In our day, we need to go after the anointing of fiery preaching that doesn't just bless, impart, and encourage but that which wields the sharp, clear, convicting power of the Word of God to confront and deliver us from our sin and compromise.

Rarely is there a true revival that doesn't address the root issue of sin, with the power of anointed preaching. The wages of sin are death and in addition to spiritually, sin produces death in many different areas our lives. How compassionate and merciful is a preacher who cares more about the lives of those reaping the fruit of sin than gaining their favour.

Revival is most often described as a fire; it's a fire of passion, fire of love, and fire of power but also a fire of holiness.

Chapter 8

Winnipeg Fire–1916

———

*"All great soul-winners have been men
of much and mighty prayer, and all
great revivals have been preceded and
carried out by persevering, prevailing
knee-work in the closet."*
—Samuel Logan Brengle

Frank Small was born into a Methodist home with a fervently praying mother. Before he was born, she covenanted with God that if He would give her a son, she would dedicate him to the Lord's service for the ministry of the gospel. He arrived, a twin, born September 12, 1873.

But Frank had other interests than being given to the Lord to preach the gospel! In fact, although he attended church, he had little interest and remained an unbeliever until he was thirty-two. His mother beseeched God for her wayward son with tears and strong prayers, yet he remained unmoved in his love of the world, music and partying.

It was a stomach aliment that jarred Small out of his resistance to the Lord. In 1906 he struggled to eat, battling an unknown ailment, at times going for weeks with only milk to sustain him. One day he noticed a newspaper announcement that a pastor from Oxbow, Saskatchewan, was coming to Winnipeg to pray for the sick. This was the authentic

Christianity that Small longed for; it's what he saw in Scripture but had never experienced: prayer for the sick!

He quickly wrote to Reverend E. W. Chrismas, the visiting pastor, and in that letter voiced for the first time his confession of faith in Christ and his surrender of his life. Chrismas agreed to meet him and laid hands on Small as he prayed for his healing. Not only was Small instantly healed, but as the power of God overshadowed him, he went into a clear vision that Chrismas interpreted for him—it was Small's call to ministry.

Within the year, in the spring of 1907, Small just happened to be passing a mission hall on Alexander Avenue when he noticed a large crowd of curious people standing at the door. A. H. Argue, the former real estate agent turned pastor had just arrived back from Chicago filled with the newly outpoured Pentecostal experience that had just exploded out of Azusa Street. Small found his way through the crowd and sat down. A number of people had been filled with the Spirit, and they were testifying and speaking in tongues. What moved Small however, was the presence of God. It was something real that he had been hungering for all his life. He said, "I was definitely thrilled. My heart said, 'There is fire here—this has a real ring!' I was truly convinced that it was of God, for one could sense the presence and power of God resting on the meeting."[23]

Baptized in the Spirit

Shortly after, along with his praying mother, Frank Small was baptized in the Spirit in a home meeting in April of 1907. The experience changed him completely and set him ablaze for the Lord. How fitting that Mary Ann Small's prayers were answered so completely, and she was blessed alongside her son when the Spirit filled them—two of the first in Canada to experience the wave of the Pentecostal outpouring that began at Azusa Street in 1906.[24]

The filling of the Spirit brought Frank Small into a deep passion and an intimate relationship with the Lord. He was stirred for revival and very engaged as an active member of the congregation that had sprung up under A.H. Argue's leadership. The call to ministry Small had received when he had been prayed for by E. W. Chrismas then became publicly confirmed as he was entrusted with pastoring the flock when Argue stepped down to leave for Los Angeles.

With revival in Winnipeg his goal, Small heard of a camp meeting to be held in California with Maria Woodsworth-Etter as the main speaker and was drawn to attend. It was a life-changing experience for him, as Woodworth-Etter, in the peak of her ministry, flowed in glorious signs, wonders, and powerful healings.

Small arrived back in Winnipeg, now consumed with a burden for revival. He sought the power of the Spirit in extended times of fasting and prayer, even going three days fasting with no sleep, continuing in fervent prayer. He was convinced that it was the power of the Spirit that brought true revival, not the personality or charisma of the speaker. Unfortunately the authorities overseeing in the assembly did not agree, so he resigned as the pastor and ventured out on his own as an evangelist in pursuit of a move of God.

Building an Altar

Through the next years, although Small served as an evangelist, his main occupation was what he called, "altar building and intercessory prayer."[25] He was completely focused on revival coming to Winnipeg. He launched the Winnipeg Pentecostal camp meetings, running for two months in the summer of 1916. Then in the fall, he sought a building in town to host the ongoing work, a place to host the presence of God. This is where the move began.

It was in a dilapidated, former Jewish synagogue at the corner of King Street and Henry Avenue where Small launched the revival meetings. The first Sunday meeting, as the makeshift sanctuary was being dedicated, he rose to read the Scriptures, and the Spirit fell upon him, knocking him prostrate on the platform. Other believers in the pews began to fall out as the glory of God filled the new sanctuary. In this motionless position, God spoke to Small of the power that was coming and his need to remain humble.

Shortly after this dramatic dedication service, God spoke to Small in a dream and instructed him to invite Evangelist E. W. Chrismas to do a series of meetings. Small obediently wrote the invitation the next day, and the night Chrismas received the letter, he also had a dream calling him to Winnipeg. Jolted awake after the dream, Chrismas got up immediately and wrote back to Small accepting the invitation.

Chrismas Returns to Winnipeg

The revival began in December of 1916, with the old synagogue packed to capacity, souls being overtaken by the power of God as E. W. Chrismas preached twice a day and three times on Sunday.

Frank Small reported, "At the altars, all that seemed necessary by way of instruction was to tell the seeker to lift their hands to heaven and immediately the power of God would fall upon them. The floodgates of heaven were opened and what a sight to behold, night after night, week after week, month after month."[26]

"One night during an altar service after weeks of the revival had passed, an intensified sound of rushing, gushing waters was heard. It was the sound of a mighty cataract. The sound continued for the space of about half an hour and then faded away. Brother Small was praying for sick people at the altar at the time. He was so overwhelmed with God's presence that he ceased from prayer with tears streaming down his face. 'Yes', he said, 'God Almighty had come on the scene—it was no longer faith but reality under demonstrations.'"[27]

"One outstanding characteristic of the altar services was," Frank Small related, "that there was no begging or pleading with people to come; as soon as we took the song book to make the altar call, it seemed

45

decisions were already made. And before the first line [of the song] was finished, the aisles were already congested with people making their way to the altar; that was a perpetual scene night after night, week after week, month after month. Many times the seekers would melt down by the power of God like men slain on the battlefield—so present was the power of God."[28]

The crowds kept increasing to the point that people who could not get in would stand outside, even in thirty-below-zero weather, gripped with the conviction of God, until the altar call, and then they'd rush in to get saved. Others would wait in the hotel next door for hours until there was room to squeeze into the synagogue, going straight to the altar and responding to the salvation call.

"Many stories of wonderful healings and notable signs also accompanied this revival," Pentecostal writer, Frank Ewart recorded. "It was disclosed that a great revival was a definite answer to earnest prayer which Pastor Small and his faithful few had been engaged in day after day and night after night for months. The avenues of approach to the mission in the synagogue were blocked with crowds, until the doors were closed and hundreds of disappointed people turned away. The most remarkable characteristic of these meetings was that they were more kindred to the revivals described in the Acts of the Apostles than anything else in the religious modern world."[29]

Moving to the Theatre

The crowds became so large that it was clear a new venue was needed so Small kept the nightly services in the synagogue but moved the Sunday services to a theatre. The first meeting was packed with an overflow crowd. The next Sunday, a larger theatre was rented and leased for the winter, but even still, many times there were as many turned away as were inside. As soon as the morning service was finished and people began to leave, the theatre would fill up again for the evening service, often filling to capacity within about half an hour.

Ten Years of Fire

After six months in the synagogue, the revival was continuing unabated, and Small moved the meetings into the vacant Knox Presbyterian Church with seated fifteen hundred. By the second Sunday, the building was packed to capacity, and the revival took on a fresh fervour. The meetings continued twice a day, with three meetings on Sunday for the next year. Eventually the daily meetings were reduced to one a day instead of two, but Pastor Small maintained the three meetings on Sunday and nightly meetings through to 1926 as the fire of revival burned hot.[30]

Chrismas, the gifted evangelist, continued to labour with Frank Small until he moved to the Knox facility and then was directed to serve in the city in other ways. To replace him, Small invited other evangelists or, at times, God would divinely send them to a meeting and they would be called into the pulpit. The preaching was typically short, with more of an emphasis on the conviction of the Holy Spirit and testimonies. Always there were glorious testimonies of salvations shared in the meetings, and many times these became the entire message.

The spirit of prayer that birthed the revival continued throughout these days of fire. Intercessors laboured in travail of the spirit for souls, their prayers often focused on particular individuals whom they would seek God for and who would eventually yield to the drawing of the Spirit.

Eventually the intensity of the revival waned somewhat, but it had been ten years in span. And through this time, God established a large, vibrant congregation. Tens of thousands of souls, encountered the love of Christ and surrendered to Him; most of these were filled with the Spirit, and also many thousands healed.

Chapter 9

Owning the Land

It's easy to celebrate what God has done and continues to do in Church of Winnipeg! Many spiritual victories have been secured in this vibrant city in the centre of Canada, both in Small's day and also today. These victories, however, have all been costly. They are the result of how so many of the leaders in the Church have invested themselves and made such a deep commitment to their city. These are not hirelings that run off when hearing the first howl of a wolf; they are ones that lay down their lives for the people of God and the destiny of revival in the city.

"He, who is a hired hand and not a shepherd, who does not own the sheep, sees the wolf coming and leaves the sheep and flees, and the wolf snatches them and scatters them. He flees because he is a hired hand and cares nothing for the sheep." John 10:12,13

Of course Winnipeg is not unique in this, and across the nation, men and women of God who have been called to a city, town, or region stay and serve through thick and thin, rather than looking for greater opportunities and greener pastures. They prayer-walk their streets, they invest in uniting the Church, they counsel the broken, they serve the poor, they preach the gospel, they pray for the sick, and they do it day after day, year after year. It's this quality of commitment to the land that God so often looks for when He is pouring out His Spirit. He looks to see who really cares.

We will never see spiritual breakthrough with a casual indifference to the city, region, or nation we live in. The reason we can confidently assert this is simply because it's the opposite of how Jesus walked. The commitment the Son of God made to the lost and dying world was (and is) our example; He gave everything as He stepped into time and space. Following His footsteps, those that would walk like Him cannot bypass the call to wholly invest their lives in a city, a people group, or a nation. This doesn't mean that an itinerant minister can't be brought in and be powerfully used of God, but it does mean that someone (or someones) needs to be on the ground and wholeheartedly investing their lives for the kingdom.

Winnipeg was honoured with the heart of commitment Frank Small demonstrated to the city. He postured himself like Jacob, wrestling for a blessing for his people, unwilling to let go of the city and the promise of God. The commitment was demonstrated by the depth of his intercession, fasting, and private pursuit of the power of God. It wasn't for selfish ambition or becoming a high profile evangelist but for the sake of souls, for the sake of God's glory.

Most certainly, a genuine litmus test of our commitment to our land is our level of private prayer for it.

A Commitment to Private Prayer

In the last few months, I've had numerous opportunities to meet with groups of pastors in different settings, and they are all expressing the same desire for their churches. They are looking for prayer to dramatically increase and for a culture of prayerfulness to develop in their congregations.

When asked, I generally share two fundamental areas that need to be established in a church to foster a culture of prayerfulness. One is a change of perspective, and the other is a change of action.

We need the understanding that prayer and intercession is for everyone, not just an elite few. This might seem like a surprising perspective change, but biblically, there is no gift of intercession. Everyone has a calling in some measure to be exercised in prayer for others (which is what intercession is). One of the most powerful ways we can love on each other is by praying. It's how the apostle Paul demonstrated his love for the churches he planted and was overseeing; he continually prayed for them. This is something we can all participate in and grow in.

Secondly, there is a pervasive weakness in prayer because we haven't been discipled to persevere. Frequently, we have allowed immature, self-centred prayer to become the norm and standard—prayer that is activated exclusively by either personal need or emotion. So few are robust and mature in prayer, and one of the primary reasons is that we've not been taught that intercessory prayer is hard work. So when it gets difficult, we quit.

Intercessory prayer is enjoyable. It's even glorious at times, but more often it requires determined effort to stay engaged with the spirit of prayer, to stay in faith, to stay in a place of caring, and it requires investing our heart, not just our time.

Effective prayer requires you focus your spirit and stay in a place of spiritual alertness, or your thoughts and attention will wander. At first most people find this difficult to maintain beyond ten minutes or so; it requires the empowering of the Spirit and a willingness to be stretched and discipled in this.

Growing in prayer requires a commitment of faithfulness that inevitably means saying no to lesser pleasures. We are called to spend ourselves to see spiritual life break out and flourish wherever we have been planted and in whatever land God has assigned us to. We may never be seen or acknowledged personally, but if we are faithful to serve and lay down our lives as our Lord did, we will be known well and honoured in heaven, which is infinitely more valuable.

But prayer is not the full sum of what's required. When asked the secret of his spiritual success, David Yonggi Cho, pastor of the world's largest church in Seoul, Korea, said simply: "I pray and I obey." Obedience is the second half of the way we demonstrate our commitment to the land. We obey whatever God has asked us to do, be it serving, reconciling, giving, building, or blessing. Our lives are not our own.

Breaking the Paralysis

We live in the age of technology, and if we are wise as Christians, we'll use all the ways technology affords us to multiply the kingdom in this age. In Redleaf Ministries, we are actively using all the technology tools we can to advance and unite prayer. We use the Internet, social media, web conferencing, voice conferencing, video, and more to network, unite, teach, and facilitate prayer. We live in an age where the technology revolution is making communication much easier, immediate, and more dynamic. This is a huge blessing for the prayer movement. But one of the downsides is that technology is changing so fast, that it's created a sense of paralysis when it comes to making commitments.

You see, there are SO many options, and the technology revolution has trained our thinking and expectations to believe that if you wait three to six months, there will always be something better released! With this in mind, how do you make a wholehearted commitment to anything?

Why would you buy an iPhone now if there will be a new upgraded version coming out in a month!?

Because of all the options and the rapid change, making commitments is becoming harder and harder. With so many choices, and potentially much better options coming very soon, staying in an "I'll-hedge-my-bets" mode is a continual temptation. But God is asking us to listen to His voice, to discern His marching orders, and to invest our lives in walking them out. We may be called to a city as Frank Small was. We might be called to a people like Mother Teresa was or to a cause like Lou Engle in his commitment to see abortion ended, but we'll never get to the place of breakthrough without knowing where we are meant to invest.

The key is really to hear God's voice in this; pursue confirmations of the call, until we "know that we know"; and then put down roots of long-term commitment. These will be tested with more glamorous, easy, or financially lucrative opportunities, but like Jesus, we can't afford to trade the call of God (even if it involves a cross) for all the world has to offer.

Living Lives Poured Out

It's clear that if we are called to a people, a region, city, generation, or nation, we have a mandate before God, and He is entrusting us with the opportunity to share in His labours, His vision, and His great compassion for that specific people. We must not be afraid of being poured out and spent. This is how both Jesus and then the early apostles walked and modeled the gospel. The call is not an enhancement to our lives; it's an altar to lay them on.

"I appeal to you therefore, brothers, by the mercies of God, to present your bodies as a living sacrifice, holy and acceptable to God, which is your spiritual worship." Romans 12:1

Revivalist John Knox, the founder of the Presbyterian Church, expressed this commitment in deep agonizing intercession as he cried out, "Give me Scotland or I die." And Scotland was indeed given to this man of fire.

Seize the Opportunity

But making a commitment to the land is not just a "pick-up-your-cross-and-follow-me" walk with an expectation it will be all suffering and hardship; no, it's also the road to extraordinary fruitfulness. Think about the faithful stewards in the parable of the minas (Lu 19:11–27). They had an opportunity to invest their master's money, but it required taking risks. They multiplied what they had been given by choosing where to invest and committing the funds entrusted to them.

The unrighteous steward in the same parable didn't see an investment opportunity that was sure enough or good enough, so he buried the coins to preserve them, fearful of loss. Like this servant, being fearful to commit, and keeping our options open will end up with us squandering the very opportunities heaven opens up for us.

Jim Elliot, the missionary martyred by the Huaorani tribe in Ecuador, lived this, and his wise counsel speaks to us today: "He is no fool who gives what he cannot keep to gain that which he cannot lose."

I'm so thankful that Canada's history is full of men and women who counted the cost and said yes to the sacrifice of a life laid down in intercession, service, and the proclamation of the gospel. We also honour our fathers and mothers in the faith who paid the ultimate sacrifice of their lives and were martyred for the Lord in our nation's history. The promise of Scripture is that if a grain of wheat falls to the ground it will bring forth much fruit.[31]

This is a promise we can depend on.

With this mantle of revival lying before us, which Frank Small wore in his day, it will take hearts that are willing to say yes to the price to pick it up. It's a price of commitment to the land, commitment to the call. In many ways Elisha illustrated this as he laid down his livelihood, sacrificed his oxen, and burnt the vocational bridge behind him. This was all done before he could serve Israel by wearing Elijah's prophetic mantle.

The greatest days of the kingdom are yet to come, but the price of being fully committed has not been reduced. There is a whole new generation being offered an opportunity to usher in a move of God in our land and among our people. The call right now is to believe for it, contend for it, and seize every opportunity to advance the cause of Christ that opens for us in this generation (1 Cor 16:9).

Chapter 10

Charles Price on the West Coast

The revival that gripped both Vancouver and Victoria on the coast of British Columbia remains today as the greatest move of God this region has seen. It began in Victoria, with an invitation extended by the ministerial to young British evangelist, Charles Price to come and hold a crusade. They had heard reports of how God had been using him in Albany, Oregon, to minister in healing and evangelism. Victoria was hungry for God, and so he came.

The citywide meetings were hosted first at the Metropolitan Methodist Church, beginning April of 1923, straining it to capacity. Two thousand sat or stood in the main sanctuary and hundreds more filled overflow rooms.

The meetings soon moved to the Willow Arena, which was built to seat six thousand. But nine thousand filled the arena, and up to as many as four thousand were turned away. These numbers by today's standards are large; in 1923 they were unprecedented for Victoria's population of only fifty-five thousand. The impact Price's meetings had on the city were remarkable!

Soon Charles Price was being compared to Charles Finney as hundreds, even up to a thousand, were being powerfully converted each night under his preaching. Healings were frequent and dramatic, and the daily newspaper reported in detail the blind seeing and lame walking.

Even those with terminal conditions were being touched and healed by the power of God.

Price also conducted special meetings for the Chinese in Victoria's Chinatown. The Variety Theatre was rented, and speaking through an interpreter, he preached and prayed for the sick. Over the course of the three-week Victoria campaign, nine thousand Chinese attended these special meetings, and at least six hundred had received Christ. What is remarkable about the extra ministry to the Chinese is that these were days where BC was inflamed with racism. In fact it was 1923 that Canada, largely because of BC's urging, banned all Chinese immigration to Canada with the Chinese Immigration Act. Yet in the face of vicious racism, the true gospel, full of love and inclusion, reaches out to everyone.

Vancouver Provoked

Across the Georgia Straight, pastors in Vancouver heard the marvelous testimonies and sent word to Price, inviting him to go to Vancouver when his crusade in Victoria was finished. They desperately wanted to see a similar revival and harvest of souls; the outpouring in Victoria filled them with faith for what could be in their city. Price agreed to come. Anticipation grew as even the newspaper highlighted the upcoming event.

"Nothing that has happened in years has so stirred religious circles like the coming of Reverend C.S. Price, an evangelist, who for the next three weeks, commencing next Sunday, will address afternoon and evening mass meetings in the Arena rink.

The Evangelist, an Englishman, between thirty-five and forty years of age, comes to Vancouver in the full flush of his greatest success, the revival campaign, which just closed in Victoria. In that city, there were several sensational cures through following the simple precepts laid down in the Bible."[32]

So the Vancouver crusade began May 2 in the Denman Arena, with seven thousand present. Many churches had cancelled their own meetings and flocked to the arena to support the crusade. Price, in full faith, announced Vancouver would see the eyes of the blind opened and ears of the deaf fully restored!

The conviction of sin was very strong, and right from the first meeting, hundreds rushed to the "penitents benches" to seek salvation. The crusade continued with two meetings a day, and thousands stopped their lives to be in as many meetings as possible. Ministers from Victoria arrived, filled with glowing testimonies of what had just transpired in their city, and the anticipation for the manifestation of God's healing power continued to rise.

Healing and Controversy

The healings, however, stirred controversy and divided the hosting pastors to some degree. Some who were influenced by the prevailing theology of liberalism had no grid for the supernatural so dismissed it as hyper-emotionalism and power of suggestion. Yet with the controversy and opposition, the flames of revival grew hotter, and now the auditorium was filled to capacity two hours before every meeting with thousands being turned away.

All in all the Vancouver meetings lasted three weeks, with additional side meetings being held for the Chinese and the "Hindus" so that interpreters could translate the salvation message. In the course of these three weeks, the total attendance in the Denman Arena was 250,000 even though the population of the city was only 175,000. The last week the number of meetings was increased to three a day so that the first attendees for a meeting would have to step over those still lying on the floor under the power of the Spirit from the previous meeting.

The Talk of the City

The revival was the big news, and everyone was aware of what God was doing for so many lives were being transformed so quickly. Whole trolley busses filled with riders would spontaneously burst into songs of praise on their routes through the city; faith was everywhere. It seemed the entire city was being faced with the question, "How will you respond to the claims of Christ?" The newspaper reported daily the most spectacular supernatural healings and even the details from the preaching, which added to the fire.

The end result of these days of revival in Vancouver and Victoria was indeed great controversy and yet, tremendous fruit. Historian Robert Burkinshaw reported these dramatic testimonies from pastors who participated: "Nearly two months have now elapsed since the Price campaign closed, and we say now without reserve that never have more wonderful and evangelistic effort been held in the city...Never was there known a more beautiful and fraternal spirit among ministers and congregations, and never has it been as easy to get men and woman to consider the claims of Jesus Christ on life and possessions...Congregations are larger; hundreds had entered the churches upon a profession of faith, spiritual life has been quickened, and there is an unusual hungering and thirsting after righteousness."[33]

While Charles Price was the initial vessel God used to trigger the revival, many other leaders were swept into the power of the Spirit, and God began to use them as well.

One example of many is the pastor of Ruth Morton Baptist, Reverend Andrew Grieve. Deeply touched by the spiritual awakening that was happening in the city, he and his wife were not only powerfully filled with the Spirit, but as they ministered to their congregation, scores were saved, healed, and baptized in their church.[34] For four months after the crusade, the baptismal tank was filled and used every Sunday.[35]

An awakened desire to pray was another indicator of the impact that revival had upon a previously lukewarm Church. In Victoria, the Reformed Episcopalian Church hosted interdenominational prayer weekly, with four hundred attending, while the Metropolitan Methodist Church that had opened the doors originally to Charles Price, saw their midweek congregational prayer meeting explode from forty to a thousand.

A Bible school and church plants were also the result of the revival, and hundreds of young people committed themselves to full-time ministry as pastors, missionaries and evangelists.

A Fight with Liberal Theology

However, the liberal doctrinal influences and a fracturing of the ministerial unity, especially in Vancouver, caused great contention between the city pastors. An inquiry into the veracity of the healings was launched in Vancouver, and although no actual cases of healing were disproved, the inquiry shifted the climate of favour so that when Price sought to return for a follow up crusade the next year; there was much reduced interest in supporting his ministry.

Nevertheless, the fruit of the revival remained, and the increase of attendance and spiritual fervour, particularly in the Pentecostal churches, was unstoppable. The fire had caught, and it was not going out in the hearts of those that fully yielded to the Lord.[36]

Chapter 11

Faith for the Harvest

*"Prayer is as natural an expression
of faith as breathing is to life."*
—Jonathan Edwards

It was in 2005 that I stumbled upon the history of the Charles Price Revival of 1923. At this point I had been in full-time prayer leadership, focusing on Vancouver, for five years, so you can imagine my surprise and delight as suddenly I became aware of this dramatic revival in the city's history. I wanted to know more and for weeks became a regular in the downtown public library's periodical archive section as I scoured the old newspapers and documents on microfiche looking for the details.

Knowing the history changed me. It changed my faith level and my boldness in prayer. If God had done it before, in such a mighty way, couldn't He do it again—wouldn't He do it again?! This revival was fresh evidence that Vancouver was not too hard or spiritually desolate for God to move, touching everyone in the city in some way. I hoped others would be stirred and encouraged as well, if they only knew the embers of fire that lay beneath their feet. So I wrote a small book that documented the story of the revival and how it impacted Vancouver and Victoria. Even nine years later, it continues to be in demand in these cities because testimonies are powerful to activate faith. I've taken most of the previous chapter from this little book, but in writing this more national account of Canadian revivals, my prayer is that faith will be triggered all over Canada to believe for a fresh outpouring of God's revival power.

Faith is a critical part of God moving in any kingdom activity. Ponder for a moment how Jesus said of Nazareth that He couldn't do many miracles there because of their unbelief. Think about this: if a city could hinder the power of God through unbelief, then obviously it could welcome and activate the power of God to move through faith.

Faith gripped these two cities of Vancouver and Victoria, creating an atmosphere where the preaching of the word exploded into thousands of salvations, healings, and miracles of every kind. Both Vancouver and Victoria were filled with faith, and Charles Price was as well.

He came into the region based on the testimony of his anointing and preached the word until there was a sufficient level of faith in the word[37] to pray for the sick. As soon as he did, miracles began, and everything snowballed. But it all began with faith.

We all need to cultivate faith in our lives, but not only that, we need to be on the alert if there is an erosion of faith because of confusion, painful disappointments, or unanswered prayer.

The Bedrock for Faith

Healthy faith is grounded on two unchanging foundations. The first is the character of God. He is good; He is always good. He is faithful, merciful, true, kind, and generous. If we are confused about what has happened and even if we thought He promised us something that didn't come to pass, we need to yield this confusion to the rock-solid truth of His faultless character. It might be a "though-he-slay-me-I-will-trust"[38] type of yielding as Job did, but we must be utterly confident and convinced that He is always faithful and true.

"Then I saw heaven opened, and behold, a white horse! The one sitting on it is called Faithful and True, and in righteousness he judges and makes war." Revelation 19:11

This is the foundation for faith. Layered on this bedrock is the second foundation that this God who only speaks truth has given us His word: the Scriptures. The Bible is eternally infallible, applicable to all generations and all peoples. So our faith is based, first on who God is, then on what He's said—His written word, the Bible.

The more we saturate our lives in the Scriptures, the more faith will arise and the stronger that faith will be. This is one of the primary reasons actually praying the Scriptures is so powerful.

However, while these two foundations for faith are unchanging, and we can throw all our weight on them, our faith is also dynamically activated by the voice of God to us personally. This is the revelation of what He's saying to us individually, or corporately. He's speaking in the context of our relationship with Him.

Revelation of His Will

God will speak to us personally granting us clarity of His will, through highlighted "rhema" scriptures—His still, small voice; dreams; prophetic words; supernatural signs; and other means. As we mature in knowing His voice, we gain confidence that what we hear is from Him, and then, based on this revelation, bold faith and prayer can erupt. The revealed will of God coming through His voice is a vital aspect of building strong faith.

However, learning to hear His voice to us personally is a part of growing in relationship with Him, which is why it is wise to seek confirmations to what we sense God is speaking and give ourselves grace when we don't quite get it right. At times we may misunderstand His voice to us as we hear it through our grid of theology, desires, experiences, and so forth, but as we persist and press in to know Him, it gets clearer.

Hearing His voice is something the newest believer can experience, but still something we are all growing in.

There are tools, which God has given us that will build up our faith, especially testimonies, which we have mentioned numerous times already. But these three foundations: God's character, the Scriptures, and then the prophetic revelation of His voice are what we need to settle in our lives to create a faith-oriented walk. Testimonies then serve to further activate.

As we look at the Vancouver-Victoria Price Revival, we need to insert ourselves into the times to catch the full wonder of what God did. This was really the first time God had moved with massive healing and harvest in the history of BC. There was no memory of God working in this way that the Vancouver-Victoria believers could draw from, yet they rose in faith.

It Took Faith

Faith was required to invite Price, and it also took faith for the Vancouver pastors to rent the arena, canceling their own meetings so they could gather together.

Big, bold prayer for these evangelistic campaigns took great faith as well. Praying for revival in these cities in the days leading up to and during Charles Price's campaigns meant believers needed to exercise "faith muscles," to believe for things they had never seen. The vast majority of the believers had never personally seen divine healing; the power of God moving or authentic revival sweep through a city.

In our day, we too have the challenge of believing for something greater than we've ever seen before and to maintain that stance of faith until it comes.

Maintaining an authentic posture of faith for revival is not always an easy thing. I've been pursuing revival throughout my whole Christian life, and I need to consistently monitor my faith level. It becomes easy to say the right things, to pray the right scriptures, and even to add the emphasis that makes the prayer sound convincing but have it empty and barren of faith.

A faith-filled prayer is a prayer that wrestles the resources of heaven into our time and space. It knows exactly what it's asking for and is locked on to it, believing that it will be obtained. It's not vague or merely hopeful. It is aware of what the Lord desires, and it is determined that it will be realized.

A prayer without active faith takes no risk; it's full of loopholes and generalities. It's going through the motions of prayer but is futile and empty without the dynamo of faith.

"And without faith it is impossible to please him, for whoever would draw near to God must believe that he exists and that he rewards those who seek him." Hebrews 11:6

If we aren't actually sure that God is the rewarder, and that our prayer will be responded to by heaven's action, we need to stop and find whatever faith we can, even if it's a mustard-seed size, and pray from that place. It's so much better to be real with our faith level and seek for it to genuinely grow and expand than to pretend. God always knows there's no shame in being honest and praying, "Lord help me in my unbelief!"

But bigger isn't always better. We can overstep by asking for more than God has directed us to pray for, stumbling into prayers of presumption. Faith is not just trying to stretch your imagination as big as you can; it's discerning what God is doing, as well as what He's poised to do, and agreeing with Him.

Grandiose prayers with good intentions but without the substance of authentic faith are just wishful thinking, even fantasy. It's the glorious substance of faith that's real because it's linked up with God's will, word, and character —that becomes a landing strip for heaven.

Faith for the Harvest

Faith is the currency of the kingdom. It moves the other gifts, and it's by faith that we step out of the natural into bringing the substance of heaven into our world—not faith in faith, but faith in God.

There is an unprecedented promise before our generation, which makes faith such a critical issue right now. It's the promise of the worldwide harvest, harvest beyond anything Charles Price tasted, but most certainly what he and other revivalists through the ages have prayed for and dreamed of.

While revival fire is blazing across parts of Asia, South and Central America, and Africa, it has not yet touched North America or Europe in a massive way, a way that fundamentally changes the percentage of believers in the land. However, this harvest won't be obtained, at least certainly not in its full potential, without a huge shift toward faith in the Church. This is an ongoing fight—to maintain faith for the harvest—a fight that many are not even aware they have to wage and so are losing by default.

Our forefathers had a passion for souls—a deep, unrelenting cry in their spirit for the lost that fueled their prayers, their lifestyle of personal evangelism and public preaching. As they gave themselves in fervent intercession, they prayed through to that place of peace and confidence that heaven had heard. From this place of victory, new spiritual life sprung forth, and they saw the very answers they had laboured for in prayer.

This is birthing prayer, travail that brings forth new life. Sadly, it's not how we in North America have learned to pray. We've either opted for light, shallow prayers that skim the surface of the need (perhaps because we're not in faith that He would answer), or we have no endurance to stay in the place of contending until the answer comes. Without endurance, our prayers end up sabotaged by distractions and discouragement. Then, undermined by false teaching that contending prayer is all striving and human works, we loose the confidence we need to wrestle with long-term faith for the breakthroughs.

Faith Rising Now

"The man who mobilizes the Christian church to pray will make the greatest contribution to world evangelization in history."—Andrew Murray

In 2007, God led the team at Redleaf Prayer to establish a nationwide house of prayer, which currently holds up to ten prayer meetings daily using live video and telephone conferencing. The heart is to link fiery ones all over Canada, in united prayer for the nation, to create a canopy of fervent prayer.

We began with praying for the Church, for leaders, kingdom business, government, for Israel to be saved, for our neighbour, America, and for justice. But two years ago, God began to unveil to us through revelation the magnitude of the harvest He desires to see reaped in Canada. It changed us.

Faith exploded, and we shook off, in repentance, the old doubt-riddled mindsets that God's best might be to save ten thousand or so, here or there, across the nation. In awe of the Lord of the Harvest, prayer began to rise for the bumper crop, for the size of a move of God that would forever change Canada. Our hearts began to burn with the vision of millions finding new life in Christ.

According to Our Faith

Do you find your heart rising with faith as you gaze over the ripened harvest fields of Canada, or wherever you live? Or has your faith shrunk back as you've encountered disappointments, delays, and discouragements? We most certainly live in days of unprecedented harvest internationally, and in this time it will be faith-filled prayer and action that apprehends the harvest for our land. If it's happening around the world, why not here? This mantle of faith for the harvest is ready to be seized in our day if we will walk like our forefathers. The Lord has been repeatedly whispering to us as we press in for this glorious harvest: "According to your faith, be it unto you..." It's time we stop limiting the miracles He can do in our land with our unbelief!

The more we have gone after this in prayer, the stronger in authority and faith our prayers have grown, and the more joy is rising in our hearts.

Strengthened by Testimonies

In this journey toward revival and massive harvest, the Lord gives us glorious answers to prayer that cheer us on to keep us encouraged. Going after national revival is the big ask, but when we see undeniable signs and wonders around us, we know we are on the right course and God is coaching us to keep running this race with full strength.

It's like the people of Israel in the wilderness journey, for whom God provided supernatural signs and answers to all their needs so their faith would be strong for what lay ahead. They were to recount these stories of God's great works so the reality of His care for them would remain fresh in the people's hearts. This would create a climate of faith and courage, enabling them to possess the Promised Land in spite of the giants and opposition.

We too, have some stories to recount. Some of the most tangible answers to prayer recently are in the realm of elections and government. Since 2006, prayers for righteousness and for godly people to be set in office, who would bring forth just policies and laws, have influenced every election. Some elections have seen dramatic, unexplainable results that can only be attributed to prayer.

The Story of the BC Election

One example, out of many, was the 2013 provincial election in BC. It was considered hopeless for the governing party to win. They had been in power eight years—the last years filled with scandals. Many of the strongest candidates weren't willing to run again, and the party was behind twenty-two points at the polls.

With a mere four-week election campaign, it looked impossible for any other result. But the opposition party was aggressively antagonistic to family values and the Lord used the prospect of them governing to call the Church into action.

Prayer was suddenly stirred and mobilized in local churches, in province-wide networks and in our house of prayer. Bold faith burst forth and created a momentum of contending intercession.

The last poll before the day of the election, however, still had the governing party trailing by nine points. It was an impossible gap to span in a few days, yet prayer rose even more. Then came the spiritual breakthrough, just four days before election day, we simply knew God had heard and answered. From that point on, we could not ask any more; we could only, in bold faith, thank God for what He was going to do!

You can imagine the celebration when the results of the May 14 election were tallied, and the governing party took the election with a greater majority than it had had before!

But that's not all, many of the prominent MLAs who had not wanted to run again had been ones that had been a part of previous investigations and scandals, and 24 percent of the new governing caucus was now made up of professing Christians! It was a total renewal of government, and the overarching prayer had been, not for a political party but to see righteousness established in the provincial government. It was a prayer that was gloriously answered.

Amazing Testimonies

We have also seen faith-filled prayer in this nation hold back floods, disband storms, and subdue earthquakes. Prayer has been the factor that has brought about the remarkable friendship with Israel, the fruit of which is that Canada is the first and only nation (at the time of writing) to receive the keys to the Knesset.

If God cares about these temporal issues, as important as they are, and will answer these prayers, how much more intensely does He care about revival, which changes eternity for millions?

Let's let these testimonies as signs along the way encourage and fortify our faith as we pick up this beautiful mantle of faith for the harvest.

Chapter 12

Latter Rain Revival–1948

In the fall of 1947, there was widespread dryness and a growing hunger in the Pentecostal movement that has been birthed in Azusa Street and found its way into Canada forty years earlier. The fire had faded, and a longing for a fresh move of the Spirit was gaining strength.

Perhaps one of the places of greatest hunger was on the prairies at a small Bible school led by Pastor George Hawtin. Hawtin had been a PAOC pastor overseeing Bethel Bible School in Saskatoon, but had to leave the denomination due to some difficulties and so moved his little flock of students to North Battleford where the Sharon Orphanage and School welcomed him, under the leadership of Foursquare pastor, Herrick Holt.

Meanwhile, healing evangelist, William Branham was filling the largest stadiums around the world and amazing people with the power of God as precise physical conditions were called out by word of knowledge, and healing of every imaginable disease was happening in the meetings.

Branham met a young Pentecostal minister named Gordon Lindsay in Oregon; soon afterward, Lindsay became his manager and arranged for Branham to hold a series of meetings in Vancouver, BC, during the fall of 1947. According to Gordon Lindsay, seventy thousand people attended the fourteen-day campaign, which was held in four cities of the Pacific Northwest, including Vancouver. The meetings were interdenominational and characterized by many hours of prayer and supernatural occurrences.

It was these meetings in Vancouver that drew the pastors and teachers from the Sharon School in North Battleford, determined that they would have all of God that they could. This little, hungry band of leaders returned to supply the spark that ignited the controversial "Latter Rain Movement, which quickly spread throughout the world."[39]

A Covenant to Seek God for More

One of the pastors who attended the Vancouver meetings, Reg Layzell of Glad Tidings, reports: "In the fall of 1947, Reverend William Branham came to Vancouver for a series of healing meetings. Many churches cooperated with the meetings, and we were all greatly impressed with his message and boldness. At these meetings, I again met with some of the brethren from North Battleford, Saskatchewan. We discussed the moving of the Lord and made a covenant: we would seek God in a greater measure in our own churches, and the students of their newly erected Bible school would do the same."[40]

The Branham meetings so inspired the Bible school that they set themselves to seek the Lord. They were longing to see the gifts of the Spirit granted to the whole Church, enabling everyone to function in God's power, rather than just a few high-profile, gifted evangelists.

Hunger Births Fasting

The commitment and hunger became intense. The seventy students that had moved from Saskatoon with Hatwin were passionately looking for more of God. The Bible School had discovered a small book by evangelist Franklin Hall, entitled *Atomic Power with God through Fasting and Prayer* (1946) and had been gripped by its contents. Staff and students alike embarked in long fasts and sought God relentlessly in prayer. One of the students wrote: "The truth of fasting was one great contributing factor to the revival. One year before this we had read Franklin Hall's book entitled *Atomic Power with God through Fasting and Prayer.* We immediately began to practice fasting. Previously we had not understood the possibility of long fasts. The revival would never have been possible without the restoration of this great truth through our good brother Hall." [41]

So from October 1947 through to February 11,1948, prayer and fasting became the culture of the school. "Sometimes we tried to study but could not go on, the desire to pray was so great. The classes nevertheless were dry and praying difficult and hard."[42]

God Breaks In

It was February 12, as the students had gathered in the largest classroom for devotional exercises. God flooded the school with His power, His presence, and His glory. He took charge. Pastor Ernest Hatwin wrote: "Day after day the Glory and power came upon us. Great repentance, humbling, fasting, and prayer prevailed in everyone."[43]

Violet Kiteley, who went on to found and pastor Shiloh Christian Fellowship in Oakland California, also reflects on the revival: "In 1948 people were drawn to an old dilapidated World War II hanger in an obscure location in subzero weather. There was no heater, only an old cook stove.

The services began daily at 5:00 a.m. and lasted ten to twelve hours. No meals were served. This was before the days of television of computers, and there was no media coverage. Yet still people came from all over Canada, the United States, New Zealand, Australia, Scandinavia, the British Isles, and India.

Some people claimed they saw prophetic messages in the sky or had dreams and visions that led them to participate in this new movement. Some said they supernaturally received the address and location of this outpouring and were compelled by the Holy Spirit to go and see for themselves."[44]

News of the revival continued to spread and so a camp meeting around the Feast of Pentecost was held with great response. Clergy and lay ministers were being impacted by a new empowerment of the Spirit; healing was flowing powerfully. Those that travelled the distance to come to the camp meetings were often profoundly impacted, receiving an impartation that activated new gifts of the Spirit in them.

Continued Outpouring

The Spirit was continuously being poured out on all who sought Him, and with the infilling came the full complement of spiritual gifts in a high level of power and activation. The leaders began to conclude this outpouring marked a new measure of the fullness of the Sprit in the Church, beyond the experience of Azusa Street. The practice of the laying on of hands was widespread, which had certainly not been the norm before the outpouring, and this form of ministry was tremendously impacting those that gathered. The whole atmosphere was electric with the power and presence of God.

Ernest Hawtin again reports: "We are reluctant to publish or even tell the following news because we know it is not believed by many people. It is true nevertheless that God is definitely restoring the gifts to the Church, and the nine gifts of the Spirit are in operation among us, both in the school and in the Feast of Pentecost. Many biting and caustic comments have been made regarding what God is doing here, but the fact remains that the sick are being healed, the devils are being cast out, saints are being edified, sinners are being saved, and we neither have the time or space to argue with unbelievers. 'Can any good thing come out of Nazareth?' Come and see." [45]

In July another series of camp meetings was held, this time with even greater attendance from around the world. Richard Riss quotes George Hatwin's account of the July meetings: "Day after day the word was taught, and then signs followed its teaching. Morning, afternoon, and evening, people were slain under the power of God and filled with the

Holy Spirit. We had been praying for a return of the days when people would be filled with the Spirit immediately when hands were laid on them as they were in Samaria and Ephesus; it was with great joy one night to have two ladies walk up before the whole crowd and receive the Holy Spirit in this fashion. When hands were laid on them one immediately fell under the power of God, the other began to speak in tongues as the Spirit gave utterance."[46]

It was here at the July Camp Meetings that Pastor Reg Layzell ministered and became involved with the new outpouring. Even though worship was integral in the revival meetings, he added an additional emphasis on Spirit led worship and taught from Psalms 22:3 that "God dwelt in the praises of His people" in a literal sense. Praise and worship were the vehicles God used to release His presence and to move powerfully by His Spirit. Spirit led prophetic song was present in every meeting;[47] worship was filled with the supernatural and became a constant priority in the movement.

Heavenly Choir

The revival spread into various centres, especially in western Canada. Saskatoon was greatly touched; Edmonton hosted special meetings in October of 1948 that gathered the various Pentecostal denominations in unity. Others, from all over North America and even Europe, attended these meetings; it was here that James Watt, a former elder in the movement, describes the first supernatural occurrence of the "Heavenly Choir."

"It was a mighty organ, with great swelling chords and solo parts weaving in and out, yet with perfect harmony. Those who heard it some blocks away said that it did something to their souls that no power on earth had previously touched."[48]

Voices and instruments that couldn't be accounted for lifted the worship into a supernatural realm. George Hatwin describes it as well: "From a little distance, it sounds like a master choir accompanied by a matchless symphony orchestra. It seemed difficult to credit that such a sound could be reproduced by human vocal organs. There is such a perfect order and timing as the mighty chords swell and roll that one is forced to concede there is an unseen conductor."[49]

Many speculated that the Heavenly Choir was the angels joining in. Singing in tongues was frequent, and it was common for individuals who were visiting from a foreign land to hear glorious praise in their mother tongue—from someone who had no knowledge of the language.

There were also special meetings in Vancouver, November 14–28, 1948, at Glad Tidings Temple where Reg Layzell pastored. Two meetings were held daily and three on Sunday. In the evening the meetings were always full, and the Sunday meetings were overflowing as the same North Battleford power and sense of holy visitation was poured out.

The revival continued into the 1950s with William Branham and Oral Roberts leading the movement and spreading it internationally. Today, although still highly controversial, it remains the roots of much of the current Charismatic Movement.

Chapter 13

Fasting That Moves Mountains

---

*"And he said unto them, 'This kind can
come forth by nothing but by
prayer and fasting.'"* Mark 9:29 NKJV

The Latter Rain Revival is one of Canada's best-known moves of God and recent enough historically that there are a number of saints still with us who experienced it. Sitting with them and listening to their stories makes it so real and shows the depth of how this move of God has marked, even defined their lives and ministries. This in itself is another indicator of the power this outpouring has had, that over sixty years later their eyes still get misty and their faces light up as they share the stories. However, in spite of its impact, it's also an outpouring that's been wrapped in controversy because of some of the teaching that came out of the movement and because of the life of William Branham who ended up in error and deception.

This book is not at all meant to be a defense of everything that happened in the Latter Rain Revival, nor an endorsement of all the teaching, but the goal is to give awareness of the tremendous things that did happen, the things that God Himself did do, even if there was frailty, human mixture, or error in the movement.

God himself most certainly broke out in the Latter Rain Revival.

It Began with Fasting and Prayer

Would this revival have come if the seventy students and staff of the Sharon Bible School had not set themselves to seek God—if they had not consecrated themselves to this purpose and spurred each other on to pursue more of God? We know God's heart is moved by our faith and hunger, and when He is moved, He responds. This is evidenced consistently in Scripture and in the history of the Church.

Extended fasts are not popular today; in fact fasting has only recently been restored to the Church as a discipline, thanks largely to leaders like Derek Prince, Bill Bright, Mike Bickle, Lou Engle, and others. But fasting is a critical component in serious prayer, in wholehearted pursuit of God, and in the lifestyle of the spiritually hungry.

"And when you fast..." Matthew 6:16

"I appeal to you therefore, brothers, by the mercies of God, to present your bodies as a living sacrifice, holy and acceptable to God, which is your spiritual worship." Romans 12:1

Fasting shouldn't be dismissed as works rather than living under grace; it could be (as could anything else we do) but doesn't have to be. In its purest form, fasting is obedience to Scripture and an act of surrendered worship. It's not essential for salvation, and many godly people never fast. In many ways it's not a "have to" but a "get to." It's an opportunity to get closer to God, to build up your spirit, and to weaken the hold of your fleshly desires. It's an opportunity many of our nation's revival fathers and mothers felt they couldn't afford to pass up. In addition to the internal work in our lives, fasting also releases the most glorious breakthroughs, personally and corporately. Think of Esther, of the story of Nineveh, or of Paul declaring he was "often in fasting" (2 Cor 11:27).

We too can enter into this place of supernatural breakthrough that the Sharon Bible School and so many other leaders in revival have modeled for us by adding fasting to our lives. The opportunity is before us. In our day and in whatever nation you are, God's desire has not waned for the lost to be saved or for the Church to be revived and matured in holiness, love, and power. He's not backed away from His intent to take nations as His inheritance (Ps 2:8) and for His kingdom to fully come on earth as it is in heaven. We can join Him in His desire with so much more effectiveness if we add the "atomic power of fasting" to our lives.

As Mike Bickle has often said, "Adding fasting to your pursuit of God will take everything deeper, faster." Can the next revival in the nation be birthed without fasting? Perhaps, but it's not likely.

If you are new to the idea of fasting or if it's not been something that has been successful in your life, maybe it's time to consider it again.

At this juncture let's add a few principles God has taught Redleaf about fasting as we have intentionally sought to incorporate it this into our lifestyle and into the culture of the ministry. We've found these principles most helpful so we can be rightly positioned to gain the most from fasting. But we would also say that we are not experts nor do we always walk in victory in our endeavour to fast regularly. Yet still, God teaches us and keeps calling us to take baby steps forward. These principles have helped us.

1. Fast frequently. The fear of starvation is deeply embedded in the psyche of all of us. We are wired to protect our bodies and to nurture them (although we certainly do get carried away with this!) When you begin fasting or if you haven't fasted for a long time, you will likely encounter anxiety around abandoning food, and the temptation will be to find a way to reintroduce some foods so it doesn't seem so severe. While there is nothing wrong with eating fruits and vegetables (the Daniel Fast), eating one meal a day or something similar, don't be driven to this by anxiety. This fear of hunger is overcome by simply choosing to not submit to it.

Many in Redleaf Ministries maintain a lifestyle of one fast day a week and/or a three-day fast monthly, with one or two extended fasts (seven to forty days) annually. This keeps the experience of fasting current. This current memory means we easily remember the increase of the presence of God, the clarity of spirit, and the aliveness of His word that fasting opened up for us. Fear of hunger looses its grip, and it stays weakened.

2. <u>Fast food.</u> Fasting media, shopping, and other enjoyable activities can be an excellent way to quiet your life to hear God deeply and encounter Him. Seasons of this are so helpful for spiritual growth and developing self-control, a fruit of the Spirit. But in a scriptural sense, this is not fasting. It may be wonderful, but fasting pertains to food. And in its purest form, as defined in both the Hebrew of the Old Testament and Greek of the New, it's straight up not eating.

In our desire to avoid this issue of giving up food, we will try to dance around it and come up with alternatives. Now, it's very real that some simply cannot fast for health reasons or because of the intensity of the physical work they do, but most of us don't fall in to that category. Most of us can fast.

In our attempt to avoid actually giving up food, we may choose a pseudofast, a fast that is merely self-denial in another area. However, we rob ourselves of the massive power and impact authentic fasting brings. Then, when faced with this lack of fruit, fasting loses its appeal completely, but sadly it's all been because we may have never actually fasted.

3. <u>Fast humbly.</u> Fasting is meant to be all about embracing humility (Is 58). However there is a great pitfall of self-

righteousness we can stumble into. Our fasts can be badges we wear to make us feel spiritually superior, rather than allowing the work of the Spirit to reveal our hearts and see how tremendously the grace of God has helped us every step.

Fasting, giving, and praying are all powerful spiritual disciplines, but all have the potential to be twisted by a religious spirit to be outward activities that hypocritically make us look good, while our hearts are far from God. Remember, He draws near to the humble.

"And when you fast, do not look gloomy like the hypocrites, for they disfigure their faces that their fasting may be seen by others. Truly, I say to you, they have received their reward. But when you fast, anoint your head and wash your face, that your fasting may not be seen by others but by your Father who is in secret. And your Father who sees in secret will reward you." Matthew 6:16–18

It's not just humility toward others but humility and surrender in our relationship to God. Fasting breaks the stubbornness and replaces it with an ease of yielding to the will of God. Make the most of this softness of heart to pray through areas you've found difficult to surrender and trust God with. Allow the work of God to develop humility in your heart to flourish in times of fasting.

So while strong, contending prayer is totally a part of a season of fasting; it can't be demanding something that has come from our own desire.

Fasting is not a hunger strike to twist God's arm; it's a place of embracing His heart and desires more than our love of food. If we go into a fast to try to get leverage with God and convince Him to do something that is our will rather than

His, we will be sadly disappointed. Or worse, He may say yes and allow us to reap the fruit of our self-will. "Not my will but Thine" should always be our posture and prayer. A season of fasting is always a good place to intentionally lay all our dreams, visions, and desires on the altar and give Him the right to slay them or raise them.

4. <u>Fast with prayer.</u> Fasting clears and empowers our spirits for increased prayer and more depth in prayer. It's not fasting alone but fasting with Spirit-fueled prayer that truly yields the most from fasting. While you may be weaker (if you are on an extended fast), you will have much greater spiritual sensitivity; don't squander this.

Set aside more time for prayer during a time of fasting; keep your spirit engaged in prayer even as you are involved in life's daily demands. Never be far from the place of prayer, especially in a season of fasting.

Extended times of fasting need to be done with wisdom, and there are some great resources[50] that give understanding on how to do this so you don't hurt yourself but actually enhance your health. Health is one reason people fast; however, for a Christian seeking God in spiritual hunger, it's not the primary focus. Getting closer to Jesus is the prize.

Jesus Fasted

The fact that Jesus fasted for forty days before beginning His ministry is a stunning commentary to the value of fasting and should be enough to convince us that we need fasting in our lives as well!

When Jesus was done with His fast, He came back from the wilderness very weak physically but spiritually mighty in the power of the Spirit (Lu 4:14). From this foundation of anointing and breakthrough, His ministry was launched and exploded in power. The staff and students of the Sharon Bible School didn't just believe that Jesus had paid the price and done the work, but they believed He set the example and that we should model our lives after Him.

For I have given you an example, that you also should do just as I have done to you. Truly, truly, I say to you, a servant is not greater than his master, nor is a messenger greater than the one who sent him. If you know these things, blessed are you if you do them." John 13:15–17

This small remnant in North Battleford got a hold of the little book on fasting, and they were perhaps novices, but their deep longing for God left them no other recourse. They launched into the desperate measure of extended fasting.

For us, accepting that fasting and prayer is a massive tool God uses for breakthrough, scripturally, historically and today, is a foundational place to start. Then, incorporating it into your life as a regular discipline is the next step. Finally, being willing to say yes to God as He calls you into extended times of fasting and prayer will set you up for being powerfully used by Him, like the Sharon Bible School, in whole new ways.

Extended Fasting—with Wisdom

Extended fasts need to be directed by God and in obedience to His call, but if we don't build fasting into our lives as a part of our spiritual disciplines, that call may not be heard, or it will feel overwhelming if it is.

Conversely, fasting out of a place of striving in the flesh to achieve something or prove your spirituality will not be empowered with the grace you need to fast, it will be extremely difficult and rarely fruitful.

There are times when I've been in a fast and completely forgotten about eating. I have gone though the entire day without thinking about it or feeling distracted by hunger. But there have been other times when it's an intense fight to keep going. Either way, grace is a critical component of fasting, and we need to draw heavily from God's grace to sustain us as we press in to His heart in this weakened place of hunger.

So here is another mantle we can pick up: the power of fasting and prayer that the leaders of the Latter Rain Revival used so powerfully to press in to God and to bring a massive outpouring in our nation. They saw, in the Latter Rain Revival, an explosion of the power of the Spirit that impacted Canada and the entire global Charismatic Movement. Could this happen again? Of course it could!

What could happen if a spiritually hungry remnant in Canada (or your nation) led by the Spirit, wholeheartedly began to fast and pray for revival? Would God move again, even in a greater, more extraordinary way, and sweep masses into the kingdom, renewing the Church in power and love?

Chapter 14

Revival Worship

Abandoned, extravagant worship has always been a hallmark of revival, for how can you be silent and not explode in praise when the level of mercy and goodness of God that is manifesting all around you is so great?! Intense worship fills heaven, as all who behold the Lord respond in awestruck adoration, so when He draws near to a community in glory and power, extravagant worship naturally also explodes.

At times worship carries a testimony that gives the Lord great glory (I once was blind, but now I see); at other times it proclaims and praises who God is (How great is our God...). Then still other times worship carries an intercessory cry (Spirit break out; break our walls down...), and as whole congregations sing, they are united and pulled into a revelation of God's desire. It becomes a way for large groups of people to sing their prayers in complete unity. Regardless of the style of sound, worship is an integral part of revival, and when true revival happens, hours and hours of worship flow with ease from awakened hearts.

As the Lord is preparing His people for revival in this hour, a new alignment between worship and prayer has developed. This has brought an appreciation for intercessory worship and a greater honour for anointed worship that can usher in the presence of God, with heavenly activity of the Spirit. Worship is becoming more than a warm-up for the preaching; in many places it's becoming the main event.

As with prayer, so many of us have never been trained in our church culture to go beyond twenty to thirty minutes of worship. We find that if it stretches past that mark, we get agitated and restless because we haven't developed the capacity to focus on the Lord for a longer period of time. Our impatience and eagerness to move on past the worship after a short time is often a symptom of our limited and shallow revelation of Christ Himself. We find ourselves bored instead of fascinated with Him. Yet sustaining worship and growing in our capacity to go so deep, so high in our praise of Jesus and stay there will in itself open up revelation of Him and encounters that we've never imagined.

He Inhabits Our Praise

One of the teachings that came out of the Latter Rain Revival is that praise creates a dwelling place for God, based on Psalms 22:3 (KJV): *"But thou art holy, O thou that inhabitest the praises of Israel."* It was this understanding that drove the passion to make His praise glorious and to sustain it with wholehearted abandon until God would come and manifest supernaturally.

And He did.

Today, the worship movement is exploding around the globe, in many different forms and with different streams, but with the common priority of being Spirit filled and Spirit led. It's worship that shuns the worldly showmanship or the ambition of getting the spotlight or promotion of the latest CD. It's all about gazing on the Beautiful One and giving Him an offering of true worship, worthy of who He is and what He's done.

Worship is wonderfully energizing the prayer movement, especially in settings where there is a mandate for day and night prayer. Worship creates a sustainable rhythm, pace, and constant refreshing. In my assessment, Spirit led worship is an essential component for successful day-and-night corporate prayer. The International House of Prayer in Kansas City has pioneered this and mentored a whole generation in the sustainable rhythms of harp-and-bowl prayer. We continually give thanks to the Lord for all He's done and continues to do through IHOP. This ministry is a profound gift to the body of Christ in our generation.

Another expression is the Burn24-7 movement, led by Sean Feucht and an international tribe of young zealots. Redleaf's been involved with the Burn24-7 movement since it launched in Canada, during the 2010 Winter Olympics. A "Burn" is anywhere from twenty-four to one hundred continuous hours of worship. It's one band after another in two-hour sets, leading the congregation into wholehearted, glorious praise, worship, and adoration.

At times there are moments when in the midst of praise, God calls for prayer, for personal ministry, for an offering, for dance, and more. But it's all by the leading of the Spirit.

Worship Can Do the Heavy Lifting

Worship enables us to break into faith, surrender, and agreement with who God is, and then as we've entered into His courts with praise, anything can (and does) happen. This is absolutely what happened during the Latter Rain Revival; the principle of God inhabiting praise was used. Our fathers went into worship with the expectation that it would open up a welcome environment for the Spirit. When God drew near, He came with the supernatural, for that's who He is.

We have many times inserted a Burn into the middle of our national conference, and two years ago Catch the Fire, Airport Campus had graciously opened the doors for us along with NHOP[51] to hold our joint conference in its facility. We had been in worship for about six hours when suddenly you could feel the atmosphere shift, and there was a sense of a spiritual opportunity that could be seized.

We began to pray for justice, I grabbed the mic and called up those that I knew could pray with faith, fervency, and understanding to lead a time of intercession. Strong prayer broke out as we contended for child abuse to stop, human trafficking to end, and for justice to come for those who have been so oppressed. After about twenty minutes, the burden suddenly lifted, and we flowed right back into worship.

The next day we were thrilled to see the headlines of the newspaper report that while we were praying, the Ontario Provincial Police had been conducting Canada's largest-ever raid of a child porn ring, just a short distance from where we were meeting! Sixty child pornographers were apprehended and arrested at the exact time we cried out for justice for children.

This is a great testimony, which points to the power worship has to open things up in the spirit. The six hours of worship through the Burn did the heavy lifting and brought us corporately to the place of revelation of what God was doing so we could step in and agree with Him in prayer. If worship hadn't been poured out for the six hours, I don't believe the window of intercession would have opened up in the same way with the same result.

If we have a heart to prepare for revival, worship needs to be a very high value for us. We need to stretch our comfort zone and train our spirits to go deeper and stay in that place of exalting Jesus, being in absolute awe of Him for extended times. It's up to us to worship, even if the worship leaders and teams are struggling; there is always a way to rise above out-of-tune instruments or uninspired song choices to express what's in our heart for the Lord. We also need to stay in that place of communion where worship can erupt from our lives easily and frequently through our daily life.

"Let the message of Christ dwell among you richly as you teach and admonish one another with all wisdom through psalms, hymns, and songs from the Spirit, singing to God with gratitude in your hearts." Colossians 3:16 NIV

Through the revivals of history, there have also been theme songs, anthems of praise that capture the essence of what God is doing, and as they are sung, they often release that same spirit of revival with fresh waves or enable it to breakout in new places. Let's pray for the songs that are written in this hour to become mighty anthems of revival that usher in the presence of God in unprecedented ways.

What could happen if we saw more and more extended times of deep, united, vertical worship breakout in the Church? Most certainly it would change the hearts of the people of God, for as Christ is exalted, He is revealed. It would awaken a burning love and a capacity to sustain a gaze upon our beloved King; it would stoke the very embers of revival.

It might begin with bringing a "sacrifice of praise," a volitional choice to worship without our emotions leading us, but most certainly it will shift to the glorious joy of worship as the Lord responds.

Times of Raw Prayer

Although it's clear that God meant prayer and worship to overlap and to move together, it's also clear that, especially in the prayer movement, we can get too focused on structuring prayer and feel we can't effectively pray unless we have a musical accompaniment.

It might help us to remember that Jesus didn't take a guitar or an iPod with the latest soaking music to the Garden of Gethsemane; He was alone with the Father—in raw prayer. While all these worship resources help, we can always deeply encounter God without them. Consider also that when Jesus was asked to teach the disciples to pray, He didn't respond with "sing this way" but "pray this way…".

So although the power and importance of worship cannot be overstated, it's not a formula, nor does it replace prayer. The important thing is we become strong in both and are able to flow into worship or into prayer, sustaining that place, under the leading of the Spirit, until breakthrough comes.

What we saw in the Latter Rain Revival was months of prayer, deep prayer that obtained the breakthrough, but then when it came, the revival was lifted to a whole new level with the explosive power of worship as God dwelt in the midst of His people.

Chapter 15

The Jesus Movement

Was there any hope for the hippies? Their disillusionment with the sterile, hypocritical status quo of the sixties drove them to challenge everything they had been raised with. Nothing was off limits—the government, the war in Vietnam, the expectation of school and then career for young adults, marriage, corporate America, church and the Judeo-Christian worldview. "Question authority" and "don't trust anyone over thirty" became mottos to live by.

With rampant and continual drug use, they "blew their minds," many holding on to their grasp of reality by a thread. Through alternate spirituality and experimenting in Eastern thought and religions, they fell into cults and deception. With free sex and immorality, they lost all inhibitions and plunged into deep brokenness and sexually transmitted diseases.

The Summer of Love in 1967 was a high point for the hippie movement, and it was that summer that the original handful of "Jesus people" met the Lord in the human chaos of Haight-Ashbury in San Francisco. That is where thousands of burnt-out, nearly destitute "love children" from all over America roamed the streets looking for drugs, for a party, for food or a place to crash (sleep). It was this little spark of salvation in the hearts of a small group that ignited a massive move of God to ransom a generation between 1967–1972.[52]

From this fresh move of God in San Francisco, Los Angles, and Costa Mesa, Jesus people began to drift north, and it was in 1969 that they ended up in Vancouver, British Columbia.

Two young women, Beth and Karen, crossed the border on a mission to preach the gospel at Simon Fraser University. They needed a ministry base and a place to live. They found out about St. Margaret's and phoned Pastor Bob Birch to ask if they would be welcomed. His response of "come over" changed the history of the congregation.

A Historic Welcome

Beth and Karen were the first of hundreds of hippies that crashed at the church, and the thousands that flooded to the services transforming the congregation as the word spread through the grapevine that St. Margaret's welcomed the hippies, both saved and unsaved.[53] Pastor Bob recalls: "I saw them getting out of the car, these two girls in their strange dress. I didn't know how I was going to talk to them. But they came in and put down their packs and took out their Bibles. There was a light in their faces, a sincerity, and I said, 'Sure, come to our church.' I wondered if I could accept them. But I said yes and the girls came to live at the church."[54]

The challenge was real. The young Jesus people were brand-new Christians with a dramatically different culture, trying to find a place in what had been a quiet, traditional community with lots of unwritten rules and expectations. How would the congregation react? It wasn't just long hair; it was the dirt, the smell, the outrageous clothes, and the behavior that were extremely challenging for traditional congregations like St. Margaret's. The Jesus people typically had little or no money and were often transient, so it wasn't just welcoming them into Sunday services. It meant caring for their very real needs, of food, housing, and discipleship.

"Revival in the church...always comes in unexpected ways..." Pastor Bob preached a few weeks after the hippies began to fill the church.

"We are seeing life from Jesus Christ breaking forth on every hand like a garden in springtime. He is leading us to worship and to love in a new way that has opened new doors of witness and service. The most significant of these doors is the door to the young people, and of these, God has led us to the Christian hippies, who are presenting us with a new challenge to love as Jesus Christ loved."[55]

As congregations like St. Margaret's, Open Bible Chapel and others said yes to the Jesus people, it released a tidal wave of salvations. A generation, hungry for God, for truth and love saw a Jesus they could connect with and ran to Him by the thousands.

The unchurched were swept into the kingdom, and in addition, the young people who had been raised in the Church also came alive with the revival. And many, even while in their early twenties, became leaders and evangelists in the movement. Revival historian Richard Riss reports: "David Wilkerson, an Assemblies of God pastor who founded Teen Challenge...estimated that there were over three hundred thousand Jesus people in the early 1970s. Moreover, these people may have had an influence far exceeding their numbers."[56] While the bulk of these numbers would be found in America and include the outbreaks in Europe as well, Canada was definitely a major participant in this wonderful youth revival.

Community Houses and Discipleship

Similar to the communes of the hippie culture, community houses sprung up to serve the new believers, but these homes came with the addition of leadership, care, and discipleship. From St Margaret's alone, ten different community houses were rented, each one with a "house parent" to nurture the young people in their faith and in life skills.

Community and evangelism together formed the heart of the culture of the Jesus Movement. Everyone was active in sharing the gospel and leading other hippies to Christ. It was truly a grassroots movement, organic, Spirit led, and unstoppable. Dozens of coffee houses for outreach opened in church basements and empty storefronts, so as hippies gathered for live folk music and organic snacks, they ended up hearing a relevant, compelling presentation of the gospel.

Testimonies were often the vehicle the Lord used the most to pierce hearts, and there was always an abundance of new, moving accounts of lives that had found peace and life in Christ.

Music as well became the sweet sound of the Jesus Movement and transformed the worship of the Church with the redeemed folk sounds of the day, rising in praise. Hymns yielded to simple, heartfelt choruses, from acoustic guitars and young voices. The music was full of life and anointing and fueled the fire of the Spirit.

But behind the scenes, leaders like Bob Birch contended for this revival in fervent prayer. Biographer Beth Carson documents this: "[He] knew that the renewal depended on prayer. 'What have we done to bring in all those people?' Birch asked in May of 1970. 'We were praying in secret; that's all.'"[57]

Prayer in Secret

It became know that Pastor Bob would spend whole nights at the church in prayer. At some stage he felt God tell him, "You must sleep only every other night. The other night you spend in prayer, waiting on Me."[58]. So Birch spent countless nights alone communing with the Father in obedience. However surprisingly, he wasn't always alone with God. At times he was the only one awake and available for the young people to talk to as they wrestled through questions and needs. So as well as Birch's time seeking the Lord, much counseling, prayer, and discipleship also happened through these nights.

Beth Carson again records an example from January of 1971 in Birch's words: "Oh how I am blessed by some of my young brothers, brought off the street, not having been brought up in Sunday school, but they love Jesus. Some of them were praying with me at two this morning, and then again at six. How I love to pray with them! God spoke to us through His word." [59]

But outside the wonderful work of God to redeem the youth of Canada, the rebellion and drug culture of the hippie movement soured, growing darker and more violent. The idealism of peace and love gave way to the reality of what is in the heart of man.

Embracing a Movement

Still the Jesus Movement that swept through North America was embraced and welcomed by those who genuinely were seeking truth and spiritual reality. They found it in Jesus. While the revival thrived in Vancouver, because of those that welcomed it, those that prayed, and its close proximity to California, there were other centres in Canada that also became hotbeds of this move of God. In these centres youth were also coming to Christ in large numbers, gathering in Christian coffeehouses, living in community, and preaching the gospel.

Here's a snapshot of that: Two teenagers simply launched a Christian club in their Toronto high school called the Catacomb Club. It touched the heartbeat of what God was doing in the generation and exploded to involve eight hundred fifty students by 1971. From the school, they moved the meetings to St Paul's Anglican Church in downtown Toronto where Thursday nights, in the movement's peak, twenty-five hundred zealous Jesus people would gather for worship each week.

As the movement through the nations waned from 1972 onward, the impact of the Spirit upon the lives He changed and redeemed remained. Many of these young, raw converts became established in the Lord, matured in Him, and are now leaders He is powerfully using today.

Chapter 16

What the Father is Doing

While Bob Birch wasn't the only one God used during the Jesus Movement, he certainly was a key leader in Canada. Others were more effective as evangelists and more charismatic as preachers, but would any of it have happened, if the price hadn't been paid in the secret place of prayer? Birch found himself a solitary figure, waiting before the presence of God for countless hours, and like an Abraham, he became an intimate friend of God who shared the Father's burden for the lost generation in that day. He was a man who would enter into the labour of God for souls, not based on a need to prove himself but solely on the basis of his intimacy with Christ.

In any generation in any nation, God is looking for these ones who will come near to Him and authentically cultivate a walk of intimacy with Him. The first and greatest commandment is to love God with everything we have, but still many struggle to allow that love to go beyond a commitment to work as his servant based on a deep appreciation for God's attributes and blessings.

Intimacy with Jesus

Yet intimacy with the Lord is completely different than knowing him and worshiping him from afar. It's much more than faithfully serving him; it's friendship. Intimacy will always involve knowing His voice and abiding in the place of communion with Him.

Consider Jesus's words to the Church in the book of Revelation: *"Behold, I stand at the door and knock. If anyone hears my voice and opens the door, I will come in to him and eat with him, and he with me."* Revelation 3:20

We typically apply this verse in an evangelistic way, inviting those that don't know the Lord to open the door of their hearts and receive Him, but it's actually a call to the Church. In fact it was originally written to the backslidden, lukewarm church of Laodicea.

It's a call to communion, to fellowship, to relationship that is intimate. It's as if we are being invited to recline with Christ at the Last Supper, the place where just His presence changes so much in our hearts, but then we also get to hear Him speak and dialogue with Him. Dining with Him is intimate fellowship with the God of Glory, and we are all invited into it. What is stunning is the choice is ours; we are the ones that need to respond to His invitation by opening up the door.

Intimacy with the Lord is the source of spiritual authority that manifests through prayer, ministry, and acts of obedience. If you are longing that your life have more impact, it's intimacy that you are really after—not for the sake of using God to get greater authority, but for the sake of being close to the one you love. Then with your heart united with His, authority increases as one of the many by-products.

This is how Pastor Bob lived; he loved the Holy Spirit and was deeply committed to hearing God's heart. He was one that kept opening this Revelation 3:20 door of fellowship.

Having Ears to Hear

Again from the book of Revelation, the Lord impressed a phrase on Bob Birch that became so alive in his spirit that it became a way of life for him.

"Let him who has ears, hear what the Spirit is saying to the church." Revelation 2:7

Having ears to hear means we are listening to God, we are communing with the Spirit, and our focus is not just on getting a blessing or encounter for ourselves. It's not self-focused but focused on pursuing God's heart and jumping in to what He is saying and doing in the Church at this very moment. It's a posture of intimacy.

This is a principle Pastor Bob imparted to many others as well. He became renowned for quoting this Revelation scripture, continually emphasizing the importance of listening before acting or even praying, but then also continuing to listen moment by moment for the Spirit's leading and respond in obedience.

It was this heart to see what God was doing and to follow Him into it that led Pastor Bob to open the doors to the hippies initially, and it's what sustained him in that decision as it revolutionized the congregation. It wasn't the safe, well-trodden path of tidy, religious Christianity, it was the willingness to obey and follow wherever God led.

The concept of being Spirit led and joining with God in what He is doing is a long-held principle of fruitful ministry. Consider some of these historic leaders, also used in revival, who have emphasized this concept:

"It is the task of every generation to discover the direction in which the Sovereign Redeemer is moving, and then to move in that direction."—Jonathan Edwards

"Watch to see where God is working and join Him[60]."—Henry Blackaby

"Find out what God is doing and bless it."—John Wimber

It was Jesus's intimate and continual communion with the Father that was the foundation for His stunningly successful ministry. He knew the Father, and He declared that He only did what He saw the Father was doing (Jn 5:19). Should it surprise us that those who found themselves in the thick of revival and moves of God through the years have also testified that they only do what the Father is doing?!

What Is God Doing in Prayer?

Although more and more churches and ministries have adopted this principle and applied it to their programs, priorities, and direction, it's also a critical principle in the place of prayer. This might be a new thought to some, as prayer is often explained as a conversation with God, and conversations involve two or more participants, each expressing what is on his or her heart, their opinions, burdens, ideas, and more. Prayer is indeed all that, but it's important to understand that there are two major forms of prayer. And each has a different purpose.

1) Communion Prayer—Our personal prayer lives should be rich in communion prayer—conversing, fellowshipping, abiding with Christ in the place of prayer. Thanksgiving, praise, unburdening concerns or fears, voicing hopes and longings are all the sounds of communion prayer. It involves praying scriptures that you've been reading and the Lord has been speaking to you through. At times the Sprit leads you into personal repentance while other times, often times, you invite more of God, His fullness, and blessings into your life. It's devotional, often contemplative, and the goal is fellowship.

2) Intercessory Prayer—This is the form of prayer where we are not focusing on ourselves at all but are serving God by contending for His kingdom to come on earth as it is in heaven. It's here we pray for the Church, for the lost, for justice, for the healing, and for the redemption of our society through the power of revival. Intercessory prayer is outward focused, and if it's to be effective, it must be Bible based, faith filled, and Spirit led. It must be aware of what the Spirit is saying to the Church, and praying in agreement with what God is either doing or specifically desires to do in this hour.

If we are seeking the power of God to shake the nation as we pray but don't ever draw near to Him, listen to His heart, or cultivate genuine intimacy with Him, we'll never be satisfied. In the same way, if we come to Him with just our minds and mouths active, ticking off our prayer list like our Saturday chores—while our spirits stay disengaged—we won't see much happen.

When we know the Lord intimately and follow Him into intercessory prayer, it's with the authority to pray what we know He desires. This is the place of supernatural, heaven-crashing-into-earth change. It's the place where, yes, anything is possible.

"If you abide in me, and my words abide in you, ask whatever you wish, and it will be done for you." John 15:7

Ears to Hear—in Prayer

Cultivating a capacity to discern what God is doing and respond in intercessory prayer is a powerful way to move into the adventures of the kingdom. When we are aware of what He is doing, we can pray according to His will, a vital element for answered prayer.

A perfect example of being led by the Spirit in prayer is a dramatic incident that happened just recently. In the RLHOP, one of our weekly prayer slots is dedicated to pray for the cities of Canada. Each week the leader seeks the Lord and hears from God which city to focus prayer on for that meeting; people join in from across the nation and pray together on the conference line in agreement for the target city to be blessed with revival.

At the beginning of June, Brant Levert, the prayer leader, felt to direct prayer for the small city of Moncton, New Brunswick. The team prayed fervently, and knowing the strength of the Baptist denomination in that region especially focused their prayers on asking God for the Baptists to be given a platform to proclaim the Word of God to the city. When their meeting was done, one of our staff, who had been in this prayer meeting, logged into Twitter and quickly tweeted: "Contending for Moncton...for fire, purity, unity & revival! May the sound of prayer & worship rise up and impact the nation."

The team had no way of knowing what was about to unfold; but God knew. He had directed them in prayer *that exact day* to cover and mitigate the terrible events that were about to erupt the following evening—in Moncton!

The next evening, on June 4, a young man strapped on automatic rifles and a crossbow with the goal to hunt down as many RCMP officers as he could. By the end of his shooting spree, three RCMP were dead, two were injured, and the entire north end of the city was on lockdown as the RCMP pursued him.

While this was a horrific incident, we are confident that the prayer actually prevented what could have been an even greater calamity. To everyone's surprise, the following day the gunman was apprehended without any further bloodshed, even his own. News outlets declared it was a miracle that they had been no more violence, no civilians hurt, and even the gunman taken alive.

Pray for Moncton

Through the whole day of lockdown, prayer rose from across the nation. Moncton became very aware that they were being carried in prayer and even Twitter witnessed one hundred thousand tweets containing the hashtag #PrayforMoncton.

A community in shock and mourning gathered at the hockey arena to pay tribute to the slain later that week. Here in this massive memorial service for the three constables, seven thousand gathered, with national leaders and dignitaries sitting in the front row. To this vast audience and on live, national TV in the midst of the service, the Baptist pastor of one of the slain officers gave an incredibly anointed presentation of the gospel, inviting all those present and watching to give their hearts to Christ—a specific and direct answer to prayer!

Many other extraordinary answers to prayer flowed out of that one incident, an incredible encouragement as we saw how the Lord unquestionably directed our prayers the day before the violence struck. We were thrilled with how He used them to minimize the impact this tragedy had and how He was able to even redeem good out of it. The city of Moncton continues to look to the Church with newfound favour, unity is markedly increased and there is new culture of "pray for Moncton."

If we are to rise into effective prayer that God can use to birth revival, it must be Spirit led prayer. We don't know how to pray as we should; we need the help of the Spirit to direct us in what to pray for but also to give us the unction to pray in a manner that is full of fervency and faith. Paul, writing in Romans, teaches us that the Spirit helps us in our weakness:

"Likewise the Spirit helps us in our weakness. For we do not know what to pray for as we ought, but the Spirit himself intercedes for us with groanings too deep for words. And he who searches hearts knows what is the mind of the Spirit, because the Spirit intercedes for the saints according to the will of God." Romans 8:26, 27

What a comforting verse! It's no secret that our prayers are weak; it's not at all a shock to us or to heaven. We don't have to pretend to be mighty and professional in the place of prayer; no, we can acknowledge our weakness and lean upon the enabling of the Spirit. He's waiting to help us.

Lord, Teach Us to Pray

Of course if we are going to draw from His help, we need to be teachable. We can't be like the stubborn three-year-old that insists,

"Me do it!" as they struggle with a task obviously much too difficult for them.

The Lord puts a unique importance on being teachable in prayer. This was the only thing that in the three and a half years of earthly ministry which his disciples asked for specific instruction in. Jesus prayed differently than anyone they had heard before, and they could feel the presence of the Spirit. They could discern the authority and clarity, the faith and the impact of His prayers.

I think of how Jesus taught in the synagogue, and the people marveled that he taught with authority, not like the Pharisees. It would have been the same listening to Him pray; no wonder they were captivated and asked to be taught this new way of prayer. For us, His disciples even two thousand years later, staying in a posture of learning, a place of being teachable is so important, especially in the place of prayer.

If we desire to be led of the Spirit in intercession, we must let go of our personal opinions, perspectives, and judgments and be willing to be a vessel for His use. We need to be sharp and alert so that we can pick up the burden of the Spirit and stay in that flow, rather than wandering off course.

"The end of all things is at hand; therefore be self-controlled and sober-minded for the sake of your prayers." 1 Peter 4:7

Discerning the Burden of God

Discerning the burden of God or what the Spirit is saying to the Church should empower our intercession with focus and clarity, not paralyze us with the fear of missing it.

If you don't know where to start, begin with praying Scripture and stay alert to the Spirit's moving as you pray. Often prophetic discernment will open up in this place as prayer begins to flow out of a sincere heart. It may be an image in our mind's eye, which we understand carries revelation of what God is doing or desires to do. It could be that another scripture suddenly and vividly comes to memory, adding more understanding, or we may suddenly experience a flush of faith and anointing as we begin to wholeheartedly pray.

Other times we just "know that we know" what God is doing.

As we move with the Spirit, we may be suddenly so aware that right then in that instant, as we are praying, God himself has stepped in to a situation and is actively moving in response to our request. Here we are, bringing heaven to earth in active partnership with our Father! This is what makes prayer so exhilarating, as we walk in the realm of unlimited possibilities and partnering with the mighty Holy Spirit.

Many call this prophetic prayer, but a better term might be Spirit-led prayer, for not everyone can identify as prophetic; but all believers can and should be Spirit led. The Spirit leads us into the burden of the Lord if we have ears to hear and if we truly desire to walk in intimacy with the Father.

The Jesus Movement looked very differently than other revivals in Canada because it was not so much birthed with a hungry and faith-filled cluster of believers praying for their region but rather God drawing the Church to enter into His burden for a generation. It was the burden of the Lord for a generation who had erupted in rebellion and who had completely lost its bearings. I was one of them, and I can attest that we needed a Saviour. The Jesus Movement is a story of a prodigal generation who pursued hedonism and lawlessness, yet remained in the heart of the Father.

It was His compassion that moved men like Bob Birch and His Spirit who drew these leaders to minister to the hippies. Perhaps again, the Spirit may begin to draw those we least expect into the embrace of the Father. If we build a walk of intimacy and listen to what the Spirit is saying to the Church, we can be right there, praying and ministering as God shows us what He's doing in a new generation.

When we think about discerning the burden of God for prayer, there is another important element: the gift of prophecy. The Lord speaks through His prophetic people with words, dreams, and visions to share with us what he is going to do.

"For the Lord God does nothing without revealing his secret to his servants the prophets." Amos 3:7

This is one of the reasons the Ears2Hear Council of prayer leaders was launched in 2006, a group that walks closely with the nation's prophets. Ears2Hear distributes the prophetic words from the Canadian Prophetic Council to the praying Church and then maintains an archive service so they can be repeatedly prayed into (www.ears2hear.ca). It's a way for the nation to hear what the Spirit is saying to the Church so we can line our prayers up with what God is revealing.

Reviewing what God has spoken prophetically to the nation through many different voices pulls together a mosaic picture and reveals His heart for Canada. It's the culmination of the words from seasoned prophets that have given us a vision of how He wants to use Canada among the nations, as well as unique gifts and roles He desires Canada to fill.

But it also reaffirms that there is another move of God, which is poised to come to this country. In fact a number of prophets have declared it will be like another Jesus Movement!

Consider a few excerpts from these prophetic archives:

"Toronto [the Renewal] was the gentleness of God, to prepare us so we won't be afraid when he comes to us in His power.

This is consistent with the prophetic words that happened in the late 1980s in the middle of the [spiritual] desert. God is going to send a revival; it will start with the Church. This revival will come in two waves; the first wave will be to the Church to heal the Church up, bring back the backsliders, renew the Church, revive the Church. But the second wave will be greater than the first one and will be to the streets.

I believe Toronto was the first wave. The greater wave of God is coming, and as I see it on the horizon, I just believe that there are things that God is doing. He's preparing the Church around the world for a great revival, harvest of souls, with healing and miracles, and this is the will of God."—Randy Clark, January 20, 2014

"Well, I prophesy to you that there is a great awaking, and it's going to go from sea to sea. And he shall have dominion from sea to sea. And God is coming; there is going to be so many sparks of revival that the devil's not going got be able to put it out. You know it's going to break out one place, and he's going to run over there and stop it and it's going to come another place.

There is another Jesus People Movement coming that's going to be greater than anything you can imagine or dream. The power of the Holy Spirit is going to break out in Canada!"—Cindy Jacobs, July 13, 2014

"I believe we are sitting on the edge of a brand-new move of God which will have of course, familiar elements but a whole new explosive manifestation of God's presence and ultimately empowerment, including new calls, etc. that will thrust us into the final and greatest harvest earth has ever experienced, preparing the way for Jesus's return."—Barbara Yoder, January 18, 2014

"I hear the Lord saying 'You will go beyond the number of salvations that have come in any move and they will multiply 100 fold.' The Lord says 'There is a move of salvation coming throughout Canada that will be reported through the news wires.'"—Chuck Pierce, August 4, 2010

"I see a wave sweeping across this land. For in days gone by, there have been moves of the Sprit that have been limited within local churches, but this wave shall go far beyond the walls of the church. It shall go into the marketplaces, it shall go into the schools, it shall go into the universities, it shall go into places of business, it shall go into prison systems, it shall go into the government!

Get ready, get ready! I see Canada on fire; I see Canada ablaze! I see Canada burning with the glory of God! Get ready, get ready, get ready!

This move of the Spirit of God shall come from Heaven. Now there will be those within the religious sector because it did not happen the way they thought it should and because they cannot control it, and because they could not put their finger upon it they will oppose it.

But do not fear or be dismayed, for the wind of heaven shall blow upon this land, and the fire of God shall fall. A great harvest shall be reaped and there shall be whole regions shaken by the fire and glory of heaven!"—Rodney Howard-Browne, February 2004

Chapter 17

Sutera Twins in Saskatoon

The 1971 Sutera Twin Revival in Saskatoon began in prayer. Pastor Bill McLeod was very concerned that his church, Ebenezer Baptist, had little or no interest in soul winning, and all he knew to do was to call the church to prayer until a compassion for souls began to stir. He saw the primary need, a need for revival.

His first step was to call the deacons to prayer, and then they began to meet every Saturday night to pray for revival—not a long meeting, but a regular weekly time. The next step was to call the whole church to attend the midweek prayer meeting, emphasizing again and again its importance, even over attending church on Sunday morning. Prayer began to grow; passion began to awaken. Soon the whole church was attending prayer on Wednesday nights and praying with wholehearted zeal.

The children who attend the prayer were led in a separate meeting, but soon they grew so strong in prayer that they didn't need an adult leader. They could fully lead their own time, full of a spirit of prayer.

Next prayer was added on Sunday nights after the service as the congregation, awakened in prayer, looked for more opportunities to intercede. Pastor McLeod then designed a "prayer wheel," breaking the week up into fifteen-minute segments and inviting the church to sign up to be on the wall for one of the slots. He was surprised when the whole wheel was soon covered, and at times by more than one person. His little one-hundred-sixty-member church had gone 24/7 in prayer!

This was also supplemented by home prayer meetings, hosted by leaders in the congregation. With all the prayer and fiery intercession, they remained true to one prayer. It was their constant cry—a simple, heartfelt "revive us!"

It was as if a spirit of "grace and supplication" (Zec 12:10) had landed on the congregation, and there was an uncommon heart for fervent prayer. One of the congregants testified about the change in his prayer life: "God woke me up, and I prayed for forty-five minutes, I used to be prayed out in five minutes, but not anymore!"[61]

The ground had been well prepared, and now itinerate evangelists, Lou and Ralph Sutera, were invited to Saskatoon to hold an evangelistic crusade. It was planned for twelve days, but the twins ended up not being able to leave for seven weeks as God exploded into the city with widespread revival.

The Beginning of the Crusade

The first service was like a dam breaking, as the altar workers that Bill McLeod had prepared to serve in the crusade were the first ones rushing to the altar to repent and confess their sins publicly![62] The pastor of the Alliance Church was also deeply touched and recommitted his life in full surrender to the Lord at this altar call. He was on fire, and the next day at the pastor's lunch, he publicly confessed his heart had been backslidden, even though he was in ministry. His humility and transparency created a landing pad for the Holy Spirit. God flooded in, and pastors wept, prayed, and confessed their need for the Lord.

With fresh, personal revival being poured out in city leaders' hearts, the crusade took off, and the Spirit of God began to move in phenomenal ways. Quickly the crusade had to move venues to accommodate the hungry crowds—first to the Anglican Church, then the Alliance then the United, which seated nearly two thousand with services running twice a day.

Still the crowds streamed in, and by the second Sunday, the crusade had to move to the stadium, where it continued for six weeks. The revival was marked with deep repentance, widespread restitution, and restoration of relationships. It's as if God heard the prayer of "revive me" and answered it deeply and specifically. Public confession and repentance was common, with the profound conviction of sin resting over the city.

We've Never Seen This Before

The daily newspaper interviewed the non-Christian police chief who said, "I'm not a religious man, but I do know the difference between normal church work and revival. And revival has come to Saskatoon; I know because people are coming in by the droves and confessing to crimes they have committed. We've never had this happen before."[63]

It was common for the meetings to contain hours of testimonies, full of transparent humility and confessions of hidden sin, even from the lips of the shyest, most-reserved people. Bill McLeod shares, "You would open a meeting with a song, and before you got to the second verse, there were forty people kneeling at the front, repenting and seeking to get right with God…People come under conviction of sin very suddenly and powerfully, and sometimes the agony is very excruciating until the release is found in Christ."[64]

Even the Sutera Twins were amazed, declaring: "There are more testimonies of restitution going on here than you can imagine. Christians are publicly getting right with God and others in a very remarkable way."[65]

One of the key reasons for the strength and speed of the revival momentum was because of the humility of the pastors. They had responded and stepped into personal revival themselves, rather than holding to a facade of a vibrant spiritual life. Pastors were struck with conviction of their need and encountered God in a way they never had. As they fully embraced this move of God, the people followed wholeheartedly.

In addition to the two meetings daily, afterglow meetings were held each night and would run as late as 6:00 a.m., as hundreds stayed to seek God and encounter the Holy Spirit. Anyone with a need could kneel at a chair in the centre and others would gather around to pray. Leaders testified that this was where some of the greatest and deepest work of the Spirit was done.

Revival Flows Through Many Churches

The spirit of revival was flowing through many churches now so that there was great unity, and many more places to receive ministry. God had truly overtaken the Church in a remarkable way; sleep, meals, and schedules all became secondary to the deep workings of the Spirit.

After investigating the revival, German author, Kurk Koch, shares this report: "Taxicab companies would receive calls for cabs to drive people to church well after midnight. Even though the cab drivers would protest, 'There will be no church open at this time of night,' the customers would insist, declaring they must get right with God. The driver would then discover, to his surprise, light in the windows of several churches at one or two in the morning."[66]

The word started getting out, and the Church throughout the nation started to take notice of the fire that had been ignited in Saskatoon. The superintendent of Alliance Churches arrived to see what was happening, and he reported: "The Sunday morning service was packed out, with thousands attending, and there was no preaching. People were confessing and testifying, and it lasted until four in the afternoon without a break." He said he had never seen so many tears in all his life.[67]

Quick Answers to Prayer

The spiritual climate was completely changing in the city as so many turned from sin and surrendered to the Lord. Prayer requests that had been agonized over for years were rapidly being answered. Everyday brought breakthroughs; everyone had answers to prayer that they could testify about. The acceleration of revival and momentum in the city grew, which led to widespread salvations. The Church became aware that when they were thoroughly revived the unbelievers around them were easily led to Christ. Because of this, people who had never led someone to the Lord were on fire and leading hundreds to faith.

Pastor Bill McLeod's original concern about his church not having a heart for souls was completely turned around, in a glorious outpouring where barrenness turned into abundant fruitfulness.

Radical Love and Honesty

Kurk Koch noted two distinct characteristics that deeply impacted him after he spent time in Saskatoon investigating the revival. One was the supernatural level of love that flowed between and from the revived Christians, and the other was the level of radical honesty that brought about the flow of confession. "Honest to God, honest to my neighbor," was the motto used throughout the revival.

Pastors stood publicly in large meetings, confessing that they had been hypocrites. Missionaries transparently confessed jealousy of others in ministry. No one was above repentance; these were signs of revival. Pride was utterly shattered as honesty and confession was practiced. Bill McLeod, in an interview, spoke of many people who were making long-distance phone calls, which would cost them up to a hundred or a hundred and fifty dollars, specifically to make confessions. Pastors had to be ready around the clock to receive phone confessions from those under the power of God's conviction.[68]

Winnipeg

The revived pastors and workers were urged to come and preach in many other hungry cities, in both Canada and the United States, which meant the spirit of revival began to spread quickly. Bill McLeod talked about the impact of the meetings in Winnipeg as an example of what many of these meetings looked like. He had just begun preaching, and even though McLeod hadn't asked for a response or opened up the altars, people began to flood to the front of the church to kneel and seek God. He continued his sermon, and soon the entire front of the church was filled, with more still coming, into the choir loft, then onto the platform around him. The hungry, the repentant, and those desperate to get right with God came. When all available spaces were filled, aware that the Spirit was still moving powerfully, McLeod requested the people sitting in the front pew, then the second and third, all vacate their seats so the seekers could kneel and continue to respond.

Holy fire, not man's persuasive preaching, was doing a work touching deep into hearts and turning lives around.

Pastor Richard Grabke of Portland, Oregon, who heard of a move of God and was interested in finding out more flew to Winnipeg to experience it for himself. He recounts: "He asked a taxi cab driver to drive him to a church. The man told him: 'This town is all upside down. The most extraordinary things are happening. Criminals are giving themselves up to the police. People don't want to do anything but sit in church. We are called out at all hours of the night to take people to church and in the early hours of the morning.'

"'Good, then drive me to a church as well,' answered Grabke. And he was not mistaken. The driver brought him to a church, which had been gripped by the spirit of revival."[69]

Pastors and workers from the Saskatoon revival were called to come share the fire in Ontario, the Maritimes, Edmonton, Vancouver, and into the United States, but even though the fire fell in these meetings as well, it remained the most concentrated and powerful in Saskatoon, where the deep well of prayer had been dug.[70] [71]

Chapter 18

The Spirit of Prayer

*"All revival begins, and continues, in the
prayer meeting. Some have also called
prayer the 'great fruit of revival.' In times of
revival, thousands may be found on their
knees for hours, lifting up their heartfelt
cries, with thanksgiving, to heaven."*
—Henry Blackaby[72]

In Saskatoon, revival began with a humble man who cultivated a spirit of prayer in his life, then in his church, which led to a great revival; it's a story we should all know well. It's a part of our national legacy and the path that was forged in Saskatoon is one that should be well lit, with many signposts pointing to it.

God is no respecter of persons. If we will walk like Pastor Bill McLeod and the Ebenezer Baptist congregation, the Father will also answer our prayers and send His Spirit. It may look very different, but He will respond to us as well. How encouraging that the prayer awakening in Ebenezer didn't start with a bang but began with common people who prayed lots of simple prayers. There were no big names or extraordinary spiritual encounters at the beginning, just faithfulness and desire. Let's glean all we can from how they pursued a spirit of prayer, which ultimately leads to birthing a tremendous revival. Let's turn our hearts and seek the same mantle of a spirit of prayer on our lives that a national father, Bill McLeod, walked in.

Cultivating a Spirit of Prayer

Prayer is universally acknowledged as the trigger, or the tripwire, for revival. But the problem is developing a culture of prayer, a grace for prayer that enables average people to testify that while in the past they woke up in the middle of the night and would pray for five minutes, run out of things to pray for, and be "all prayed out," but now, with a spirit of prayer resting on their lives, it's totally different. Now, it's like a torrent of prayer has been opened up in their souls, and they pray for forty-five minutes without stopping or finding it an effort. Such is the difference the Holy Spirit, manifesting as a spirit of prayer makes in a life or in a community.

In the Red Leaf House of Prayer, we've tasted both of these realities of praying with a great empowerment of the spirit of prayer and when this is at a low ebb. By far, praying with the spirit of prayer upon us is the place of exhilaration, anointing, and great grace; it's like running downhill or lifting the sails to catch the wind. It's glorious. However, there are times when it's not quite like that; in fact the wind seems still and oars come out.

We structure our prayer meetings for an hour each, gathering people to pray together from all over the nation using technology, namely, video and telephone conferencing.

There are times when, I hate to say it, prayer bogs down, and the sails are limp. It's hard going, and we may not sense the grace or anointing to pray at all. The prayer runs dry, and even knowing what to pray for becomes an effort. But as I write this, these times are becoming sparser, and the norm is where prayer absolutely erupts—full of faith, fire, and clarity of how to pray. Many times it's like the gusher of the spirit of prayer has been opened up, and time flies by. An hour is over so quickly, and we feel we could easily continue on for another two or three.

I'm very thankful that these times of anointed prayer continue to increase. They are absolutely electric, and God responds with the fruit of undeniable answers. In addition, we can sense in the spirit the changes that are happening as we contend together for God's kingdom to increase in our nation. But if we weren't faithful in the slogging times when there is little sense of anointing and were simply being obedient, I don't think we'd be seeing the grace of the spirit of prayer in our midst that we often do now.

The biblical principle of being faithful with little, and also the principle of stewarding the talent you have been given, are critical principles for cultivating a spirit of prayer. All believers are invited to pray, to bring their requests to God, and to access His throne of grace. Those that do and that keep praying, even when it seems hard or boring or even futile, will reap the reward of faithfulness, which is, of course: increase.

It's not that they've earned it, but they have cultivated a place in their spirit for a spirit of prayer to be welcomed, honoured, and hosted.

While this involves self-discipline, what is more important is a heart full of love for the Lord. When we love him passionately, there is a motivation beyond ourselves to serve Him and see His desires fulfilled, and this draws us back to consistent prayer. The questions in prayer that get asked are: "Jesus, what matters to you? How do you feel about this?" It's knowing His heart that drives us to prayer.

Bill McLeod did this: he touched the Father's heart for the lost and out of that, longed for revival. He prayed, and he prioritized prayer in his church. When they began they may have been reluctant; we could expect there were many dry prayer meetings and dry prayers. But as they persisted, something caught. Something awakened. The spirit of prayer began to empower the prayers of the saints at Ebenezer Baptist in a way they had never experienced before.

Luke 18 records the famous parable of the persistent widow with the opening statement that *"Jesus told this parable so men would pray at all times and not loose heart..."* This is so important. If we persist and allow the Holy Spirit to lead us and teach us as we pray, we too are candidates to host a mighty spirit of prayer in to our lives and churches. But, if we lose heart, give up, or get distracted with lesser things, we forfeit this incredible opportunity and privilege.

The Privilege of the Throne Room

Often as I go to prayer, I am genuinely in awe of the privilege God has given us to partner with Him in this way. Before the new covenant and the work of the cross, Israel was the only nation that had God living among them, and even then their access was so limited. Only one priest, once a year, was able to stand behind the veil in the Holy of Holies. Now, because of Christ, we have been given full access at anytime, day or night, to the Father. We are invited right into the most epicentre of power in the universe: the throne room. If that's not stunning enough, we not only have unlimited access and welcome to the throne room and presence of God, but we have His ear. We are invited to approach and speak, not just watch in awe.

We have been given such an immeasurable gift in Christ's finished work on the cross, and one of the most important aspects of that is our position of righteousness in Him, which gives us unfettered access to the Father. How sad if we rarely use this access! How great a price was paid for this and how tragic if this gift is sparsely used and marginally valued!

With the continual call to prayer throughout Scripture, both in direct exhortation and in example, it's clear that this is a role that God wants all of us to be active in, and one of the chief reasons is that it's such meaningful labour. It's so amazingly fruitful. He wants our lives to count for eternity so he calls us to prayer, for in this throne room experience of intercession, we can literally shift nations as we partner with him.

At times we think of prayer as an empty religious duty and forget how intensely potent it is. If we remember the nature of our Father who has called us to be prayerful people, we realize that he would never ask us to waste our lives on anything futile. During the Second World War, the prisoners in the Nazi war camps were forced to spend their days in futile labour. They filled wheelbarrows with dirt and dumped them on one side of the camp then reloaded the dirt again, wheeled it across the camp and put the dirt back where they got it. Day after day they did this. The futility led to despair, which led to a high suicide rate.

God is the exact opposite of this; He honours us with the most fruitful and meaningful labour- labour that has the potential of eternal impact and fruitfulness.

When we reflect on the story of Ebenezer Baptist, we may never know if the truth of the privilege of prayer awakened them or if they simply started praying because their pastor prayed and called them to follow him as he followed Christ. One thing was obvious, however: everyone was expected to be an intercessor.

Are You an Intercessor?

In our Western Church, sadly, most people wouldn't call themselves intercessors. Somehow we've come up with a unique designation for the people who like to pray that we call intercessors, but the rest of the church doesn't identify with that role. There has even been, in recent days, lots of teaching that intercession is a special gift of the Spirit like an apostle or a pastor. While this teaching was likely developed with the best of intentions to honour those labouring faithfully in prayer, it doesn't have a biblical basis so ends up with really negative side effects. Here are three of the most obvious ones:

1) If we don't identify with being an intercessor and encounter dry, uninspired times of prayer, we assume this confirms our lack of gifting so don't apply ourselves to exercise faithfulness in prayer to allow our prayer lives to develop. Of course giving up on prayer leads to widespread prayerlessness, and the Church is thus robbed of the power of the Spirit, as well as so many other blessings.

2) Those that are discerned to have the "gift of intercession" are often delegated the bulk of the prayer. They then can become swamped with requests and burdens, which they can't possibly carry, or they have to skim through them instead of deeply engaging and praying through a need. The end result is many fewer blessings, breakthroughs, and victories for the Church.

3) Those that don't feel they are intercessors bypass deeply exploring the fellowship of Christ in the realm of intercession. This is an exquisite place of His presence, communing with His heart, and receiving revelation of His will, which is untapped by those that never press in beyond the veil in prayer.

But in Bill McLeod's church, they didn't make this distinction. Everyone was called to prayer, even the children. They stayed at it until it began to flow and multiply, and it got so anointed they added more and more times of prayer.

Andrew Murray said it well: "Where there is much prayer there will be much of the Spirit; where there is much of the Spirit there will be ever-increasing prayer."

Another key point is that they also stayed on task. Bill McLeod reports that they had essentially one prayer request, "Revive me, O Lord," and they kept laying this request before God. While they did take prayer requests weekly for the needs of the congregation (and saw weekly answers), they kept constant in this posture of contending for revival. It's similar to Evan Robert's famous prayer of "Bend me," rather than praying for anything and everything that could be thought of. They knew what God wanted and stayed determined in prayer until He answered. They were a perfect example of the persistent widow, for whom even an unrighteous judge would respond and grant justice.[73]

The perseverance of prayer that Ebenezer Baptist found is something most pastors would love to see in their congregations, yet it is quite rare. More find the church prayer meetings struggle with being dry and sparsely attended. Eyes frequently glance to the clock to see how much time is left in the meeting. Sharing needs, requests, prophetic words, and exhortations take up much, if not most, of the time to compensate for the weak prayer muscles that we've let atrophy.

Corporate Prayer that Stays on Fire

Yet there are ways that prayer can be strengthened as a congregation seeks to welcome a spirit of prayer in a greater way. After years of going after this, we have stumbled on five essential elements that we see contribute to cultivating a sustainable fire in a corporate prayer meeting, be it in a house of prayer, a local church, or other community. These are all beautifully illustrated in Ebenezer Baptist's journey into the spirit of prayer.

1) Intimacy—If each participant walks in a deep communion with the Lord and abides in His presence, as they join together in corporate prayer, they will find an ease with flowing into the direction of the Spirit. They will naturally pick up the Lord's desires and the life of the Spirit.

However, in any church or house of prayer, there is a great diversity in levels of maturity, experience, and intimacy with God. You obviously can't legislate this or expect everyone to be at that same place. But you can build a core of leaders that can keep the prayer on course and model this Spirit-led prayer. One person leading who has a mature, intimate walk with the Lord won't be enough to create this synergy; often he or she will find himself or herself shepherding the prayer to keep it from straying instead of facilitating the flow of the Spirit. Synergy requires a team. A team can model and establish a culture that others naturally begin to step into.

Without intimacy the prayer doesn't just go off course, but the faith level will sag, as well. You find the language of prayer getting stale and religious, ringing hollow with empty clichés but no heart. We end up praying merely out of our thought life, our ideas, and opinions, rather than flowing under the inspiration of the Spirit.

2) Community—So often people come to prayer to pray with their friends or those that inspire them. It's a place of very meaningful connections, a place to find someone to carry the burden of God with, and a place where we see in a very real way—a multiplication of the fruit of our labour.

"Two are better than one, because they have a good reward for their toil. For if they fall, one will lift up his fellow. But woe to him who is alone when he falls and has not another to lift him up! Again, if two lie together, they keep warm, but how can one keep warm alone?

"And though a man might prevail against one who is alone, two will withstand him—a threefold cord is not quickly broken." Ecclesiastes 4:9–12

While building community and relationship is important, it's also important to keep intercessory prayer focused outward so that our prayer meetings don't become all about us. In that place there is still a very real fellowship of the Spirit and joy we share in consistently praying together. In RLHOP we have some teams that have been in prayer weekly with predominantly the same people for over seven years. Many times, it's the people we pray with and our growing relationship with them that encourages and gives us the heart to be consistent in prayer.

People who exude joy and faith and walk in victory will always be people that others will want to pray with; their life in the Spirit is contagious!

3) Prophetic Vision— *"Where there is no prophetic vision the people cast off restraint"* Proverbs 29:18. This scripture is engraved on Canada's Peace Tower at the Parliament

Buildings so has, perhaps, a unique importance and application to this nation. Having a prophetic vision, the sense of what God is doing right now and has promised to do is what mobilizes and prioritizes prayer. It keeps it fresh and immediate.

The prophetic vision, however, is bigger than just words of prophecy. It's the principle of having ears to hear what God is saying. It's discerning the times and seasons and praying from that perspective. Prophetic words may at times play a key part in this but not always.

Prophecy and prayer are cut from the same cloth in many ways, and it's not uncommon for prophecy to be given in times of prayer. This can focus and invigorate prayer wonderfully but only if the prophetic word is accurate. It's unwise to adopt everything that's spoken without the guidance of discernment. Soulish prophetic words can actually hinder the prayer, by shifting the focus into fear, criticism, or odd rabbit trials. A good rule of thumb is that prophecy should be for edification of the body of Christ (not the prophet). This means, the prophet is postured to serve what God wants to do in the time of prayer, by adding to the flow, bringing clarity, encouragement and illumination. Genuine prophecy will awaken faith rather than fear.

That said, it's also vital to recognize emerging prophets often feel very vulnerable stepping out, and they need to be cared for and affirmed, even if their word wasn't helpful.[74]

The compelling prophetic vision that burst Ebenezer Baptist into prayer was that the fullness of time for God to pour out His Spirit in revival was upon them! He was looking for a willing vessel. The word may not have come to them with a fiery presentation from a renowned prophet, but it settled into them as a faith-saturated revelation. It bore witness in the hearts of those gathering to pray. They knew this was what God was doing in town.

4) Answers—How exciting it is to testify of exact answers to prayer—even more if they came in the moment you had interceded! For many people this is the bottom line, and it's seeing the frequent answers to prayer that invigorates prayer meetings. Conversely, with seemingly no answers, many get disheartened and slip away from the discipline of corporate prayer. If we kept record of what we prayed for, we'd quickly see how many more prayers are answered than we'd ever expected. A typical person will forget much of what was prayed for without some kind of note keeping, so this is an excellent help to tracking the fruit of prayer.

Also praying prayers that are measurable will give you an opportunity to see the impact that prayer has made, rather than only praying prayers that are vague or general.

For example: In prayer last week, we were interceding for pastors and leaders in our nation who had been encountering severe spiritual attack. We felt a very strong sense of leading in this direction, so we energetically pressed into it. But then the prayer got more exact, and we prayed for the leaders of a specific city, spending considerable time lifting their arms like Aaron and Hur, as they stood through the battle they were facing. Within a week we had two separate conversations where we heard wonderful testimonies of significant breakthroughs from two different leaders in that city. It's likely there were many more leaders God helped, but hearing blessings that came to these two was a great encouragement.

5) Faithfulness—Lastly, prayer, like any kingdom activity, requires commitment. It requires a choice of our will to make it a priority. If we are weak in our commitment, we will

find ourselves being led by our emotions. We'll encounter continuous reasons why going to the corporate prayer meeting is inconvenient, and our attendance will be spotty at best. Never has there been a move of God birthed out of casual comfort and convenience; rather, it's zeal and sacrifice that mark its inception.

Faithfulness, or commitment, will be tested. It always is. But when it's passed the test, blessing, and breakthrough, authority and increase are released.

If we have all of these features in our corporate times of prayer, we will definitely see it flourish. We'll have a prayer meeting, which is not just sustainable but thriving, growing in fire and momentum. At Ebenezer Baptist they saw all of these in abundance: intimacy, community, vision, answers, and commitment. These kept the church steady and increasing in the passion for prayer.

However, for most, we are not experiencing a high level of fire and momentum in corporate prayer. So the place to begin is where we are. We begin with faithful obedience, nurturing the spirit of prayer, first of all in our personal lives, then as an overflow, in our church community. If we are faithful and follow His Spirit in obedience, we can trust that Galatians 6:9 applies to us, and the reaping we'll see is the answer from heaven to our cry for revival.

"And let us not grow weary of doing good, for in due season we will reap, if we do not give up." Galatians 6:9

Chapter 19

The Beauty of Repentance

"The sacrifices of God are a broken spirit;
a broken and contrite heart,
O God, you will not despise."
—Psalms 51:17

Another major feature of the Saskatoon Revival was the wave of confession and public repentance that broke out everywhere. It was as if the light of God, pouring into the region made it intolerable to hide sin. Holiness became irresistible. Kurt Koch, who witnessed the revival called it "radical honesty," and reported that arrogance, self-seeking, and pride were the most frequently confessed sins in the public settings.

This is almost foreign to where most congregations are today. In our current Church culture, repentance is viewed very negatively. It's associated with groveling, punishment, God being angry, shame, failure, performance, and on and on, even though bringing us to repentance is one of the ministries of the Holy Spirit. In fact repentance is actually glorious, even though it can be painful at the time; it's the welcome course correction that's vital for kingdom life to flow.

Imagine if you had a severe food allergy to gluten and didn't know it. Your life was filled with debilitating medical problems and pain, and despite many doctors and medical tests, you couldn't find the cause.

Wouldn't you want to know that it's actually all because you ate gluten regularly? To know that all you had to do to be pain free would be to adjust your diet would seem like very welcome news to most people. Maybe some would want to keep eating gluten in spite of the consequences because they loved it so much, but most would instantly abandon it, just glad to find out what had been hurting them.

Repentance is like this. It's giving up behaviors, attitudes, or thinking that hurts us because they are sin and sin reaps death (Rom 6:23) in so many different ways. But unlike the gluten-free diet that is popular today, giving up sin is not depriving us but redirecting us to the path of abundant, joyful life. It's God's grace to reveal sin to us, because sin is so destructive and separates us from Him. It's wisdom to invite the conviction of the Spirit into our lives so we can see where we may be entangled and compromised in sin.

"Nevertheless, I tell you the truth: it is to your advantage that I go away, for if I do not go away, the Helper will not come to you. But if I go, I will send him to you. And when he comes, he will convict the world concerning sin and righteousness and judgment." John 16:7,8

"This is the message we have heard from him and proclaim to you, that God is light, and in him is no darkness at all. If we say we have fellowship with him while we walk in darkness, we lie and do not practice the truth. But if we walk in the light, as he is in the light, we have fellowship with one another, and the blood of Jesus his Son cleanses us from all sin. If we say we have no sin, we deceive ourselves, and the truth is not in us. If we confess our sins, he is faithful and just to forgive us our sins and to cleanse us from all unrighteousness. If we say we have not sinned, we make him a liar, and his word is not in us." 1 John 1:5–10

Sadly we often misunderstand and think of repentance as God nitpicking and accusing us of failures and shortcomings; we even confuse conviction with condemnation. There is no condemnation in Christ Jesus, but the Lord will use conviction to bring things to our attention that are not conforming to Christ-likeness and then simultaneously extend to us the grace to repent and change. How desperately we need an ongoing fresh and deep revelation of the Father's heart of kindness toward us, of Jesus's commitment as Redeemer, and of the Spirit as our Sanctifier.

When God brings sin to light by the work of the Holy Spirit, it is not for the purpose of grinding our face into the dust and condemning us as a failure. Instead it's out of the immeasurable, deep compassion and kindness in His heart, longing to set us free from sin and all its destruction. Sin brings a breech in our intimacy with God. It opens the door in our life to darkness and demonic activity, and it yields terrible fruit of brokenness (not the godly kind of brokenness) in our lives and the lives of others we impact. The impact of sin, even if forgiven and cleansed, can carry on for the rest of our lives. It certainly did with King David. There is no upside to sin.

Entrenching in sin and refusing to respond to the Spirit's wooing to repentance will require us to harden our heart to Him and to deafen our ears to hearing His voice on the matter in question. Continuing down this road leads us to drift further and further away from His presence and his grace.

The Pharisee Road

At times we may want to hold on to a sin we consider particularly pleasurable and yet maintain our reputation of spirituality. This is a step toward hypocrisy, living a double life. It's setting a course down a road that leads to becoming a religious Christian, one with an outward show of righteousness, but an inward life of darkness. This is how the Pharisees ended up in such disastrous spiritual condition that Jesus in his great love, had to attempt to shock them into conviction.

"Woe to you, scribes and Pharisees, hypocrites! For you are like whitewashed tombs which indeed appear beautiful outwardly, but inside are full of dead men's bones and all uncleanness." Matthew 23:27

"And he said to them, 'Well did Isaiah prophesy of you hypocrites, as it is written, "This people honors me with their lips, but their heart is far from me; in vain do they worship me, teaching as doctrines the commandments of men."'" Mark 7:6,7

Perhaps you thought that He just didn't like the Pharisees and was really rude to them because they opposed him! No, that wasn't it at all. He was certainly grieved that they represented God to the people in such a distorted way, but he was also deeply grieved with the darkness they had fallen into personally as they deceived themselves. Pride will always lead to deception. Deception often requires more extreme confrontation to breakthrough its proud resistance.

Jesus looked at the Pharisees with as much love as He had for those whom they condemned as sinners, but He recognized the hardness of their hearts. He understood how trapped they were in their confident assertions of holiness and their dependence on the outward show of spirituality with the respect and power it gave them.

A man or woman God uses must be willing to walk in sensitivity to the Spirit of God, even when he comes with conviction of sin. In the midst of a Spirit of revival, repentance in the Church abounds, and because of it, freedom, joy, and restoration of relationships also abound.

The Alliance pastor who took the first step and shared vulnerably of his backslidden heart in the midst of the pastor's lunch gave leadership to a movement of repentance that revival rode in on. He didn't consider his ministerial reputation as important as responding in wholehearted, deep repentance when God shone His light of conviction on his heart. Others may have felt the same tug, many others were likely in the same spiritual place, but this man of God had the humility and courage to lead the way. The wonderful thing is, that when the pastor did, thousands followed! He became a father of revival that even we can learn from and emulate in this generation, as he mentors us with his example into humility and transparency.

David's prayer of should be a part of the prayer vocabulary of any Christian:

"Search me, O God, and know my heart;
Try me, and know my anxieties;
And see if there is any wicked way in me,
And lead me in the way everlasting." Psalms 139:23,24

Asking God to search us, weigh our motives, and reveal to us any sinful ways is a prayer that will keep us soft, teachable, and convictable by the Spirit of God.

Public Confession and Repentance

In the Saskatoon Revival, repentance went deeper than just a personal contrition before God. It went public, as repentant confession was featured in every meeting. It also flowed out of the church as mature Christians and new believers alike, in this spirit of repentance, practiced restitution. Restitution signals the fullness of repentance. It's beyond just being sorry; rather it's choosing to walk the opposite direction, even if there is a cost.

Restitution, for those that might be unfamiliar with this practice, is going beyond even a heartfelt apology, taking steps to make things right in whatever is possible. Often where there has been theft, cheating, or corruption, restitution pays back and makes whole those that have been wronged. Zacchaeus gives us a beautiful example of the sincerity of his repentance with his pledge of restitution here:

"And Zacchaeus stood and said to the Lord, 'Behold, Lord, the half of my goods I give to the poor. And if I have defrauded anyone of anything, I restore it fourfold.'" Luke 19:8

But not everything should be confessed publicly! Obviously there are wise boundaries of discretion that should not be crossed when allowing for public confession. No woman appreciates a Christian brother standing up and confessing that he's been lusting after her!

Clearly there are things that should be confessed in a private setting or just kept between the individual and the Lord. The principle of wisdom that many pastors and leaders use is: confession should be made in the circle of injury. So if someone's sin has impacted the whole church, confessing before the whole church is appropriate. But if it's a private matter between a married couple, or between a few friends, public confession is likely not necessary, nor advisable.

With wisdom and good pastoring, confession that gives glory to Jesus for His delivering work, not glorifying the sin or confessing for the sake of personal attention but true Christ-honouring confession is an amazingly powerful tool that God will use. It so often opens the way and gives courage for others to follow, allowing them to also gain their freedom.

Public confession demonstrates to everyone the vulnerability and temptations that are common to man, and it creates a point of accountability, a place of pivot, where a new direction has been set in a memorable way. It helps us fully turn from sin and walk in that new way.

If we are to walk in revival and be carriers of revival in our land, the sensitivity to the conviction of the Spirit and an embracing of a lifestyle of quick, wholehearted repentance needs to mark us. Pride creeps in so easily and subtly that we need to refuse to submit to its ways and stay real, vulnerable, and humble, both before God and our brothers. This is a life that God can pour out upon one who loves the approval of God more than the empty praises of men.

Not Manipulation

Revival begins with the Church and it's about the life of God flowing with supernatural power into the Church as a result of a restoration of intimate relationship between God and His people. So when conviction is present, repentance should be welcomed and made room for. But there is a great difference between conviction of the Spirit and the religious manipulation to get a response of repentance.

True conviction has a sharp prick to it; it's like a light going on to a sudden awareness of attitudes, words, thoughts, or actions that displease God. They are plainly before us, and it's easy to see where we have transgressed. Manipulation that is meant to create a show of repentance is filled with fuzzy accusation and leaves you feeling generally unworthy and condemned. Ask the Lord, "What should I have done differently?" If the response from the Lord isn't clear, wait on Him to deepen and clarify the conviction or to show you that it's a spirit of accusation at work. The work of the Spirit in conviction leads to life; it's filled with hope, redemption, and God's presence.

I remember being in a meeting a number of years ago where the speaker had been peaching about Canada's abortion record and then called the congregation to be awakened in passion for this injustice, which is a massively important message.

However, the speaker felt it was also important to make sure there was a passionate response to the message, so called those over thirty years old to find a place in the room to get with God and to repent for allowing the legalization of abortion in Canada during our watch. For me the problem was that I had been a child when the laws changed so couldn't be expected to have taken responsibility, and then as a young adult, I became deeply committed as an activist for the pro-life cause.

This made repenting for indifference or not taking responsibility quite a challenge! There was very little sense of conviction in the room, and I remember asking the Lord, "What could I have done differently?" Still the pressure from the pulpit mounted, as the response wasn't forthcoming, and I clearly wasn't the only one struggling with this. Then finally, after multiple exhortations and an extended period of time, in frustration, the speaker pulled a few ladies to the mic that seemed to be generally complying with the kind of response that had been expected. They instructed the ladies to pray repentant prayers on behalf of the rest of us, which they did to the best of their ability. Perhaps they had genuinely been under the spirit of conviction, but it seemed more like they knew what was expected and were performing accordingly.

I left that meeting feeling grieved and somewhat heartsick with what had transpired. It seemed the strong desire for an emotional response from the congregation was more motivated by the speaker's need for tangible results and less about what God was actually doing.

I'm sure this isn't the only time when a speaker's personal needs led them to step across the line into hyping or manipulating the audience in the flesh. I'm sure most speakers have struggled with this temptation or crossed this line in their zeal at one time or another; I know I have. However, while we don't want to move in the flesh, we also don't want to resist even the faintest or lightest conviction of the Spirit. God shouldn't need a flashing neon sign or loudspeaker to get our attention.

In a similar way to the disciplines we recommend for fasting, keeping "short accounts" is an effective spiritual discipline to keep religious pride, with its cold heart and deaf ear, from getting a foothold. When the conviction of God touches your heart, be quick to repent, quick to confess and make it right with whomever you may have wronged. Resisting and delaying this will make it all the more difficult to do so; it strengthens pride and conviction can fade. As it says in James: *"God resists the proud but gives grace to the humble."*[75]

If the urgency of conviction isn't obeyed, frequently the next step will be to dismiss the conviction and carry on, even though a lifting of God's presence may result. The Lord may in His grace bring conviction back to us in an increased way so we are again aware of the need to address the sin, but if we refuse to respond or do so in a superficial way, we risk distancing ourselves from Him.

Many times when Christians struggle to hear God's voice, it's because they did not respond to the voice of the Holy Spirit that spoke to them about a need for repentance. We can't pick and choose what God speaks to us about; we can't tell Him that bringing conviction to us is off limits, while we want to hear His encouragement and affirmation of us. If you have struggles hearing God's voice, this might be the issue. Ask the Lord to show you if you closed your ears to Him as He was seeking to bring an issue to the light in your life. If He shows you something, repent, ask for His forgiveness and cleansing, and choose to live a life more welcoming to the correction of God.

God is holy, and while we are positionally clothed in Christ's righteousness, our sanctification is a work in progress. So this means that repentance should be a part of all of our lives. It's a point of recalibrating our lives to line up with heaven's direction, priorities, and values. It's a natural part of growing to become more Christ-like.

In a pursuit of revival, authentic repentance should be something we are quick to embrace, even welcome into our midst. So if conviction begins to move among us, let us respond with courage and genuinely contrite hearts, with radical honesty, just as our fathers did.

Chapter 20

The Father's Heart Revival

Perhaps the greatest, most globally impacting revival in Canada's history is the most recent one, that which has been known as the Renewal, the Father's Heart, or the Toronto Blessing.

Beginning in January of 1994, at Toronto Airport Vineyard (now Catch the Fire), this massive outpouring has spread with profound refreshing, restoration of hearts, healings, and joy, through the whole body of Christ. In many circles it has brought a seismic change of how the Church actually views the Father. With that change, serving the Lord out of grit and determined obedience has yielded to a new walk of receiving, being filled and empowered, and then giving away God's love.

The revelation of the Father's love has been revolutionary. It's a warm, intimate, affirming embrace that has lifted the burden of performance and brought deep healing to hundreds of thousands of hearts. It has resolved deeply, long-buried issues of rejection and abandonment, freshly establishing lives into the height, depth, width, and length of the love of God. This revelation did not just come with new teaching and emphasis, however; it came with extraordinary power.

This is the power of the Holy Spirit that manifested by sweeping through meetings where great swaths of people (hundreds at a time) were slain in the spirit and, in that place, personally encountered God in life-changing ways. They were ministered to, touched, and filled with Him. Joy was common; uncontrollable laughter would break out and overwhelm meetings. And in the midst of it all, people would be set free, healed, and restored.

Inviting God to Come

These were days and meetings in which you never knew what to expect other than God would show up, often with the simplest of invitation: "Come Holy Spirit" or "More Lord." When He came manifestations of His work in hearts took the form of being slain in the spirit, spiritual drunkenness, "crunching" (being bent over), jerking, shaking, or crying out. Even those who were attending the meetings with the intent to observe and critique would often find themselves overcome with God's presence and undone by His love.

The power and love that God poured out was more than any man or woman could control or withstand without intentionally hardening their hearts.

International Hunger Awakes

The renewal brought the hungry and thirsty from the globe. Nightly meetings sprung up quickly after the outpouring began and carried on six days a week for twelve years. Through these days of revival, from all over the world, millions found their way to Toronto to partake of what God was doing. But it wasn't just an international gathering of the thirsty; it also broke through denominational walls. The work God was doing was transforming so many that denominational flavours, styles, and preferences were no longer barriers.

For the first time in the body of Christ, denominational affiliations became completely irrelevant, and believers of all stripes stood shoulder to shoulder at the altar receiving prayer ministry and experiencing God. This was a revival that celebrated the inclusiveness of Father God, and there was room at the banqueting table for everyone, regardless of theological persuasion.

As revival always does, it began with hunger.

The Arnotts' Journey

John and Carol Arnott, who pastored Toronto Airport Vineyard, speak of how in the early 1990s they found themselves worn out with seeking to respond to the never-ending demands of pastoring. In this place of weariness, they attended a Benny Hinn Crusade in Toronto during the summer of 1992, and the power of the Spirit present reminded them that this was the missing component for fruitfulness.

With a freshly awakened hunger, the Arnotts dedicated their mornings to meet with God in worship, prayer, and the word. The Lord deeply met them with a restoration of first love and a new confidence that there was much more of God to be had. In John Arnott's words, "We fell back in love with Jesus in this precious season of our lives."[76]

In pursuit of more of the power of the Spirit, they travelled to Argentina to witness the revival that was engulfing that nation. They attended the powerful crusade meetings led by Carlos Anacondia and visited the Almos Prison (an institution completely transformed by God), but the power fell when Carol Arnott was prayed for by Claudio Freidzon. She was overcome by the power of the Spirit, and along with manifestations of spiritual drunkenness, she received a fresh impartation of faith for miracles and a move of God.

As the Arnotts returned home with hope and expectation, they became aware that Randy Clark from St. Louis, also a Vineyard pastor, had been pursuing the power of God as well and had recently been greatly impacted when prayed for by Rodney Howard-Browne. They decided to invite Clark to Toronto to do four nights of meetings in late January 1994. The outpouring began the first night as Clark simply shared his testimony and invited people up to receive prayer. It was on these hungry ones, in a small, humble church that the Spirit of God fell.

When word got out that God was moving, there was no holding back the crowds. What started with a small meeting of a hundred and twenty from a church of about three hundred sixty saints saw the congregation multiply tenfold—with thousands nightly attending the renewal meetings.

Explosion of Fruit

Twenty months later, in an accounting of what had transpired to that that point, it was recognized that six hundred thousand people had attended the nightly meetings, including twenty thousand Christian leaders and two hundred thousand first-time visitors. [77]

There had been over nine thousand first-time commitments to Christ, as well as countless healings and lives filled with the Spirit afresh.

Today, as the Father's Heart Revival has just passed its twentieth anniversary, pastor and revival historian, Jerry Steingard reports: "Aside from thousands of new churches, dozens of new apostolic networks, thousands of new ministries or existing ministries that now operate at a whole new level of anointing and countless hearts, bodies, and marriages healed, we have seen at least several million converts throughout the world."[78]

With the fire and the power came, not surprisingly, the controversy. The manifestations that accompanied the moving of the Spirit were everywhere, and some were extremely bizarre. It's quite understandable that many pastors, leaders, and even denominations were very concerned, to the point of distancing themselves from the holy chaos that had broken out. So while on one hand this revival powerfully brought unity among the hungry from the nations and across denominations, simultaneously, it brought the heartbreak of division in the Church.

The practice of soaking became paramount for sustaining the fire. This was waiting on God in a heart posture of receiving His love. It became a regular, daily practice for those involved in the movement, and was a continual source of refilling.

Soaking mobilized hundreds of presence-saturated workers, which kept the fire alive and growing.

Catching the Fire

One of the remarkable features of this revival was the transferability of the outpouring. Within a year from the beginning of the outpouring, it was estimated that four thousand churches in the United Kingdom alone had been impacted by the Father's Blessing, as well as thousands of congregations across Canada, the United States, and Australia. Notably in Canada, Kelowna, Winnipeg, and Saint John were among the hottest spots, carrying the same intense fire and power of God. The typical scenario of this revival transfer would begin with a dry leader attending the meetings in Toronto where he or she encountered the Father's love to the point of a radical transformation. The next step would be the leader returning home to "give it away," imparting to others what they received through the laying on of hands, who in turn would impart to still others.

In this way, the renewal was transferred to Holy Trinity Brompton (HTB), an Anglican church, as Eleanor Mumford, wife of John Mumford, pastor of the Southwest London Vineyard, spoke and ministered in May of 1994. Steve Hill, an Assemblies of God evangelist, also had a tremendous encounter with God at HTB and went on to become one of the key leaders of the Pensacola Revival in Florida, which began on Father's Day 1995.

Brenda Kilpatrick, wife of pastor John Kilpatrick, came to be refreshed by the Spirit earlier that year. She was totally renewed in her love for the Lord and intimacy with His Spirit. Through this conduit, the Spirit moved, and the Brownsville revival broke out. This revival was similar but with a different focus, and through this outbreak, 134,000 salvations were recorded as over 3.5 million people from all over the world flocked to the meetings.

Another notable transfer was through the missionary couple, Roland and Heidi Baker of Mozambique. Arriving in Toronto weary and desperate for God after sixteen years of difficult missionary work, Roland and especially Heidi, had power encounters with God that radically changed and empowered them with the Spirit. Hours, and even days, of "carpet time" resting in God's presence, soaking Him in, allowing Him to minister to their hearts. Receiving His love transformed and empowered them.

Today the Bakers give leadership to Iris Global and have planted well over ten thousand churches, care for tens of thousands of orphans, oversee massive feeding projects for the poor, and have established a Bible school. Their network of pastors regularly sees the dead raised, the blind having regained sight, and the sick and broken healed. They are changing their nation.

Of course, Randy Clark, one of the original pioneers of the revival, has continued to carry this anointing for signs and wonders all over the globe, giving leadership to Global Awakening. This is how his ministry recalls the outbreak of revival:

"After months of prayer and fasting, Randy got touched by the Lord mightily. And, on January 20, 1994, this unassuming pastor from St. Louis walked into a small storefront church near the Toronto Airport. Originally scheduled for four days, his meetings have turned into a worldwide revival that has impacted millions of people!"[79]

Jerry Steingard interviewed Clark in Toronto during September 2013 for his book on the revival, entitled: "From Here to the Nations: The Story of the Toronto Blessing"[80]. During this interview, Clark cited three examples of ministries that were launched or significantly impacted by the revival and had gone on to lead over a million souls to Christ each. He mentioned the Bakers in Mozambique, but also Henry Madava in Kiev, Ukraine and Leif Hetland of Norway, who ministers among Muslims in the Middle East and Pakistan.

This is all fruit, which has touched nations through the magnitude of the Father's Blessing, poured out initially in Toronto. While these are some of the more notable examples, the impact of countless lives that have found a new intimacy with God through this revival has changed the Church. However, even with all of this, the prophets associated with the revival declare that a greater wave of God's power is still to come.

Chapter 21

Honouring the Spirit

Choosing to not control the seemingly way-out manifestations that erupted during the most intense days of the Father's Heart Revival in Toronto was very costly, but it revealed a commitment to honour the Spirit and submit to His lordship in the revival's leaders. This heart to honour the Spirit and to continually seek to host the Presence, avoiding anything that would grieve Him, was a nonnegotiable in this revival. It meant that God had the latitude to work in glorious, deep ways that wouldn't have opened up otherwise. He transformed hearts as His power was unleashed in the meetings large and small and also in personal encounters.

It meant Arnott and the other leaders needed to break rank with any religious conformity and refuse to bow to the fear of man. Traditions and practices (even if they were more modern) had to submit to how the Spirit was moving. This is easier said than done. The fear of man is a very real pressure, even a demonic spirit, and it exerts much control in the Church. The refusal to compromise and yield ground to this spirit always becomes costly; it was for Jesus.

"And He answered and said to them, 'Why do you yourselves transgress the commandment of God for the sake of your tradition?" "So for the sake of your tradition, you have made void the word of God. You hypocrites! Well did Isaiah prophesy of you, when he said: "This people honors me with their lips, *but their heart is far from me; in vain do they worship me, teaching as doctrines the commandments of men."'"* Matthew 15:3, 6–9

Traditions don't have to be old, historic rituals that have endured for centuries; they can simply be entrenched habits that we are comfortable with. They've become our ways. We don't want to change them; they suit us. Traditions aren't at all negative. Many carry the rich revelation of the Church's history, but the issue is when the ways of man refuse to submit to the Spirit of God.

The fear of man also tries to exert pressure through the expectations and opinions of man. These too needed to be laid down in the holy chaos of the Father's Heart Revival.

Soaking

This nonnegotiable of honouring the work of the Spirit also meant the new concept of "soaking in His presence" was developed and became a marking feature of this revival.

Soaking is an intentional posture of the heart of receiving the Father's love, affirmation, and touch. It's recognizing we all need to experience God's love and that He delights, as any father would, to communicate it. It's a place of deep communion, worship, and intimacy. In the revival meetings, bodies were often strewn on the floor or standing and swaying with eyes closed and cupped hands outstretched in a "receiving position" as God did unique works and ministered personally to thousands at the same time. Thirsty and dry souls simply soaked God in.

A new genre of worship music even emerged as the practice of soaking and resting in the Spirit for extended periods of time was enhanced with the prophetic musical sounds.

Abiding Bears Fruit

It's difficult to adequately describe the revolutionary change that has occurred in the Church through the development of this value of widespread honouring the Spirit and the practice of soaking. It has for so many rewired their hearts, their concepts of God, and the nature of their relationship with Him. It has brought the Church back to the place of deeply abiding in the Vine so that vibrant, kingdom fruit can burst forth and remain. It has renewed the joy of relationship, just being with Him and knowing Him, has risen as a higher priority than labouring for Him. The Lord has restored the Mary heart of sitting at His feet to the Church who had, like Martha, become driven with the busyness of ministry and the needs of the world.

While soaking in the context of a meeting is not as common today, the practice of soaking in personal devotions remains a feature of the walk of the believers that have gone on to bear revival fruit throughout the nations.

The two most intimate human relationships we commonly know are the bond between a parent and child and the bond between a husband and wife. The Lord uses both of these as illustrations to express the depth of His heart for us to know Him and walk with Him. We don't have to prove anything to be His beloved; Jesus has done it all. Still this good news often seems too good for our religious orientation, and we continue to expect to have to somehow earn His love. Soaking in His love, in His word, and in His Spirit is the continual place of being filled with Him and keeping our religious bent at bay.

As we daily enter into His presence; speak to Him our love, worship, and adoration; and listen to His heart, the chemistry of our hearts is changed. Here, the insecurities, fear, and shame fall off, and we are able to live in that place of being loved—going on to love others freely. This is primary in the practice of soaking, it's above all, being with Him and communing with Him. It requires time and letting go of what we expect, so He can be free to speak or move upon us as He wills. It's the practice of genuinely honouring the Spirit in our personal lives and, then as we gather, honouring Him in our midst.

Let's look as some of these features of honouring the Spirit in a bit more depth.

Give Him His Place

A symptom of our lack of relationship with the Father has been our polished church machine that functions very smoothly without Him. We've learn how to work with human nature to motivate and organize people as well as any secular organization. We include God's word and His causes, but sadly we have so often closed the door to fellowship with Him personally.

The unpredictability and power of His Spirit scares us; He's not a tame God that will stay in the tidy administrative box we've constructed for Him. As the Scriptures say: *"Who of us can dwell with the consuming fire?"*[81] Then, how do we walk intimately with the Almighty? To avoid this glorious, terrifying adventure of faith, we often pull back to what we deem a safe distance, and instead of letting Him lead, we take the reins of control to guide a church or ministry. We may even draw back to such a distance that we don't even wait on Him for direction but only include Him when it's time to ask for a blessing on all our plans and efforts.

In contrast, honouring the Spirit means we yield the primary leadership of all we do to Him. We trust Him and surrender to Him. We no longer walk like Saul, wanting to impress the people with our leadership and willing to go on without inquiring of the Lord, indifferent to His presence. We instead, like Moses, set the highest value on His presence. We recognize He's the most excellent leader, so listen and respond to what He does in our midst. It might mean He chooses to move in a different way than we would expect, so we yield and adjust. In fact it very often means our plans need to be yielded, submitted and adjusted.

We must give Him fully the place of leadership if we are to genuinely honour Him, for the Church is His people, His family, His body.

Give Him Time

Lingering in His presence, allowing Him time to do what He desires, both in our personal walk and in our corporate gatherings is a powerful way to honour the Spirit. If we were hosting a high-ranking dignitary, we would most certainly seat him or her prominently, ask them to speak and give them the freedom to fully express their heart without cutting them off. The goal is honouring the Holy Spirit so He is given the prominence He deserves and is thoroughly welcomed, however He desires to move or speak.

However, welcoming more of the Spirit is not simply moving through a meeting slowly or jettisoning structure in favour of spontaneous free flow. The kingdom is full of structure, and God is well able to inspire planning, even if it's put in place months before the event. The issue is to stay in the place of listening, communing, and responding to the presence of God and His leading, even in the advance planning process.

Structure should always serve the Spirit, not become the master.

Give Him Value

Worship is the response of a heart that truly values the Lord. It's the cry of "worthy, worthy, worthy" erupting from the hearts of His people—a hymn that will never be silenced or get stale. Worship must be recultivated in our lives if we are to welcome and honour the presence of God in fullness. But let it be worship that is focused on Him, not primarily singing about us, our journey, or how He makes us feel. There may be a time for that, yet our purest worship will always be utterly Christ centred.

Give Him Our Hearts

The pursuit of God's presence and Spirit is not a new concept. Moses, David, Mary of Bethany, and John all stand out as ones who longed to just be near Him. They were a part of the company of countless hidden ones who through the ages have loved Him and pursued His presence as their highest treasure. For these ones, worship is no effort; service and even great sacrifice are the natural outflows of hearts that have been utterly captivated by Him.

"Whom have I in heaven but you? And there is nothing on earth that I desire besides you. My flesh and my heart may fail, but God is the strength of my heart and my portion forever." Psalms 73:25,26

The greatest issue of honouring the Spirit of God is that we love Him—with all the intensity of passion that a human heart can bear. We love His presence, in however He comes and manifests, and while He deeply satisfies the soul hunger, at the same time, He awakens a glorious yearning for even more. Loving God then abides as the eternal, fiery heartbeat of all revival.

As we love God wholeheartedly, we cannot separate Him from the things He loves and values. It's not just about magnificent, intimate fellowship with Him, as wonderful as that it; it's also welcoming others, whom He loves so much, into that union.

The famous motto that came out of the Father's Heart Revival was to "Walk in God's love and then give it away," simply and clearly capturing the call to the great commission as an outflow of intimacy with the Father. It's loving Him in a way that what matters to Him and what brings Him joy becomes our great mission and burning passion. It's loving Him in a way that the great commission becomes both great in preeminence and focus and a commission that marks and motivates our lives with holy purpose.

Our Response

Chapter 22

Let Justice Roll

Whenever the topic of revival comes up, it's almost inevitable that someone will voice the objection: "We don't want visitation! We want habitation!" or "We're not after revival; we want transformation!" This reveals the deep longing for more than a flash-in-the-pan experience, which fades and seems to leave no permanent change—or worse, even a deteriorated condition in our community.

When we look around at our communities and nation, we see an overwhelming need for God—for His redemption, wisdom, justice, and reformation. Surely these needs would be addressed with the fire of revival. Surely if God is moving in power, justice and reformation will also increase! But it doesn't always seem to happen that way.

Revivals have frequently been aborted before they were able to mature into full-blown societal reformation. But even though reformation hasn't always been achieved, it doesn't mean that there hasn't been lasting fruit. Every life that has been touched through a move of God, every soul saved, every marriage restored, and every drop of heaven's dew is to be treasured. The fruit of Canada's revivals is all around us; it runs deep, like veins of gold in the history of this land. You simply can't separate the journey of the Canadian Church from the outpourings of God.

That said there is a very real concern when a community experiences an outpouring of God's Spirit and never really changes in character. We grieve when hearts that were awakened and overflowing with God's love and power end up relapsing to their former coldness, or even into a worse condition of cynicism. Casting away the faith and passion, and becoming sour to the call to revival, they skeptically say, "been there, done that." It's as if they've been inoculated by a shallow experience to the pursuit of genuine, deep, heaven-crashing-in revival where God changes everything. With this in mind, we would all agree that we have to contend, work, and pray for more than a temporary experience. The goal is permanent, powerful change that becomes an earthly reality of the kingdom of God.

Perhaps we have been too quick to call something a revival. Perhaps the vital place of repentance and the need for a heart to deeply encounter the power of the cross have been something we have glossed over, or bypassed all together, at great cost. Conversions that don't stick, lifestyles that don't change—these end up being a reproach to the name of Christ.

Return to the Cross

The cross is always an offense; it offends every culture, in every generation. We will always be tempted to soften its demands for a complete surrender and to avoid mentioning the power of the blood or the fact that there is no other name by which mankind can be saved than Jesus. These realities raise the hackles of our culture, and we know it.

Charles Finney, one of the greatest leaders of the Second Great Awakening, wouldn't give an altar call until he was convinced the conviction of the Spirit was at the level people needed to fully embrace a place of wholehearted repentance and full surrender. Have we lowered that bar too far?

So even though we welcome any level of God's blessings and the moving of His Spirit, let's posture ourselves for pursuing more. Let's pray for the greatest outpouring of His Spirit this nation has ever seen, an outpouring that leads us to the cross.

In addition, let's preach and teach the work of the cross as a forever demonstration of God's love and mercy and also as the place that we are called to in unreserved surrender. Self-life can be suppressed, and it can be dressed up in different ways to fit in. It can endure temporary behavior modification, but it will always sprout back up like uncontrollable weeds. The only way to permanently deal with self is submitting to the work of the cross.

Let's teach once again that true Christianity has always been about Jesus being our Lord, not just the source of our blessings.

When I Survey the Wondrous Cross[82]

When I survey the wondrous cross
On which the Prince of Glory died
My richest gain I count but loss
And pour contempt on all my pride

Forbid it Lord that I should boast
Save in the death of Christ my God
All the vain things that charm me most
I sacrificed them to His blood

See from His head His hands His feet
Sorrow and love flow mingled down
Did ere such love and sorrow meet
Or thorns compose so rich a crown

Were the whole realm of nature mine
that were a present far too small
Love so amazing so divine
Demands my soul my life my all

Justice Rolls Out of Revival

A life that's been marked by the cross cannot be oblivious to the needs around us. If we say we love God and are happily disengaged from our world, we are deceiving ourselves. It's in the seasons of revival where reformation and justice should take the biggest strides forward. It's when hearts are the softest that the fear of the Lord the strongest, and entrenched traditions and alliances are all in upheaval. With the backdrop of revival, the slave trade was broken, women gained the vote, and prisons became much more humane.

Similar to the need for justice in the days of the Great Awakening, we also have profound issues that desperately need to be addressed. However, the passion for justice should not be in competition with the pursuit of revival, but rather, justice and reformation will naturally spring forth as revival awakens a multitude of hearts, igniting a massive shift toward loving our neighbours as ourselves.

We must realize as well that we are wrong headed if we look to government to resolve our society's needs for reformation. Government is not our saviour, nor is an elected government the equivalent of an Old Testament king, who is able to do whatever he pleases and decree laws, based on his personal morality. In a democracy, the people are more the "king," for they can choose their prime minister or president and remove them if they are not satisfied. While the government does have a measure of power, it is limited and temporary.

This is why we can't merely seek political power by electing Christians and expecting them to legislate Christian behavior or values against the will and culture of the majority. No, we are not Crusaders. If we achieved that goal, we would simply drive sin temporarily underground for it to rise with greater rebellion and aggression at a later date. This is not true reformation.

Although we do want righteous laws, our goal is not this kind of surface change, so we must contend for the expression of reformation that springs as the fruit from hundreds of thousands, even millions, of gloriously converted hearts. These will be hearts that seek just laws for the unborn, for the First People, for the poor, and for the honouring of religious freedom and family because they now know Christ and know what matters to Him. The strength of this movement will enable government to make sustainable changes towards justice, for the reforms they bring in will be backed up by the heart of justice in the people. This should be the full fruit of revival.

We must pray for government, for we are biblically mandated to do so. And as well, we need to be active in the public arena. The influence of the people of God, with a biblical world-view serves a salt and light to promote righteousness, justice, mercy, and godly wisdom. But we must remember, the lead influencer of a nation is the Church, not the government. The greatest authority rests in the hands of the Church, not the elected or appointed officials.

We are not a remnant of refugees, like Daniel and his friends trying to survive in the demonic kingdom of Babylon. We're not keeping our heads down, quietly praying for the peace and prosperity of the city, as we wait out our term of exile. No, we are the advancing ecclesia of God warring for the salvation, redemption, and reformation of our nations. We are the people of God for whom the gates of hell itself will be no resistance.

So let revival roll into our nations and go so deep and wide that countless hearts will be utterly transformed by the power of the cross like John Newton, the slave trader who met Christ and wrote Amazing Grace to describe the depths of his conversion.

But while revival may be the best time to move forward with breakthrough on issues of justice, does that mean we simply wait and pray until then? No, not at all! We must be engaged and active for we are called to do good works, even in seasons when the rains of revival seem only like a distant whisper of a cloud. We are accountable to stay engaged, be vocal and visible as we speak for justice and righteousness, even in times when no one seems to hear. There will be a day for the breakthrough of reformation if we stay faithful.

Although everything in us should be in earnest pursuit for revival, as beautiful as it is, it is not our final goal; it is merely where we must begin. Reformation (or transformation) is the next stage, but beyond both and encompassing them all is the kingdom of God, which is greater, more glorious, and the fullness of what Jesus desires on earth. Revival and reformation both contribute to the kingdom of God being established and manifesting in fullness. On earth as it is in heaven.

The Gulf Oil Spill

When considering how revival and reformation complement each other, here is an illustration we often use that helps to make it clear:

In April of 2010, a deep-water oil well in the Gulf of Mexico, owned by British Petroleum, blew out, and over the next three months, five million barrels of oil spewed into the ocean from the wellhead. It was on the nightly news, and the frustration of all involved, and of us who watched helplessly, was palpable, as the oil slick grew in the Gulf and the flow continued, day and night from the bottom of the ocean.

There were two critical components to the response to mitigate the damage. There was a crew that went to the wellhead with submersibles and sought to seal the well, to halt the flow of pollution. But there was also another large crew that was responsible for containment and clean up. They were tasked with protecting the fragile ecosystems of the Gulf Coast from the devastation of the spreading oil. They used floating booms, skimmers, and dispersant agents to stop the spread and clean the water as well as they could.

Like this illustration, we need to be concerned with the heart of a person (the wellhead) but also the impact of their sin (the containment). On a larger scale, while we need to have primary concern for the hearts of the people of our nation, and minister to hearts through the gospel, we still must give ourselves to cleaning up and containing wickedness, through acts of reformation.

"For from within, out of the heart of men, proceed the evil thoughts, fornications, thefts, murders, adulteries, deeds of coveting and wickedness, as well as deceit, sensuality, envy, slander, pride, and foolishness. "All these evil things proceed from within and defile the man." Mark 7:21–23

Both are critical and play a role, but the priority always falls on the heart. It's only by turning hearts that the flow of wickedness slows, and without heart change it continually increases and multiplies.

With this clear priority in place, the Church thrives in our role to be a voice for justice and a doer of good works. Here is where the world sees the heart of God in deeds as well as words. Caring for the poor and oppressed, seeking reformation of unjust or unrighteous laws, supporting marriage and the family, fighting for the sanctity of life from birth to natural death, stewarding the environment, protecting and educating children, welcoming immigrants—these and more are all areas that the Church has a role to play in as salt and light in society.

Demonstrate God's Heart

It's through doing good works and being actively engaged in our society that we demonstrate God's heart and His ways tangibly.

However good works also mitigate the devastation of wickedness. Sin brings death to a soul, but it also leaves a trail of broken lives. You only have to look at a family that has been shattered by the infidelity of one of the parents, spiraling into an acrimonious divorce and a broken home to see the collateral damage of sin. Sin leads to broken lives and wounded hearts, and wounded people wound others.

Wickedness also opens doors to demonic influences and welcomes the increased oppression and activity of demonic spirits. These evil spirits entrap lives into all manner of bondage and deception, increasing the hostility to God and the multiplication of evil.

When we consider the call to reformation held in tension with the call to revival, the tension is resolved with saying yes to both, but the greatest priority is given to revival and the redeeming work of the cross upon the hearts of men. This must be so because the hearts are where wickedness begin, but it's also so because everything must be considered in light of eternity. It's easy to lose this perspective with the clamour of pressing needs all around us, but all our labour and priorities should be held up to this plumb line, the plumb line of eternity. With that in mind, salvation is the highest priority in any setting.

"Lord, stamp eternity on my eyeballs."—Jonathan Edwards

But the question we floated at the beginning of this chapter remains, "How do we sustain revival long enough and enable the work to go deep enough so that it blooms into authentic societal transformation?" I'm not sure if anyone in the Church is fully qualified to answer this definitively. But certainly, as we've reflected on some of the most significant revivals in the Canadian journey, some clear dos and don'ts emerge. Let's look at these.

Unity

A huge key for revival to be sustained and authentically transform a region is unity. Particularly at a leadership level, relational unity is the container for sustaining revival. The type of unity that is forged over years of relationship, honour, love, service, prayer, forgiveness, and not giving up when things seem impossible. This unity is Jesus centred, not merely political alliances for the sake of the outward appearance or for ministry opportunities.

Jesus knew this when He prayed in the Garden of Gethsemane in His last hours of ministry before being handed over to sinful men. He travailed for His bride; He agonized in prayer, birthing the Church—His ecclesia commissioned to bring heaven to earth. Everything He asked for in that pinnacle of prayer matters intensely, but if you look closely at this prayer in John 17, you'll see the highest priority is on unity. Let's look at these verses that so reveal His heart:

"Keep them in your name, which you have given me, that they may be one, even as we are one." John 17:11

"That they may be one, just as you Father are in me and I in you..." John 17:21

"The glory that you have given me I have given to them, that they may be one even as we are one." John 17:22

"I in them and you in me, that they may become perfectly one..." John 17:23

Revival can break out without widespread unity, as we see with the Canadian stories, but it won't be sustained without a leadership team who is deeply united at a heart level. Charles Price was a classic illustration of this; all of Vancouver and Victoria were being awakened with the power of God, yet the leaders of the Church in Vancouver allowed division to enter and entrench. Eventually the division created too much opposition to the move of God, and Charles Price was essentially run out of town.

In the midst of the amazing crusades, he had seriously considered moving his ministry base to Vancouver. It seemed a city so full of hunger and faith, a city where he had initially great favour, but then it turned against him, primarily because of division.

Unity that can withstand the pressure of revival must be both Christ centred and come from the heart. It will be severely tested, and the close-knit relationships of leaders who are able to stay accountable, transparent, humble, and together steward what God is doing are most frequently established before the move of God breaks out.

Christ-centred unity means we all yield to Jesus's leadership and set his kingdom as the highest priority. In this place we can graciously give and receive correction, we all lay down personal ambitions and agendas, and make room for and value each part of the body of Christ that is also yielding to His lead.

Man-centred unity looks different. It's potentially a larger group, but there is a mixture of motives. While there can be a great heart to advance the gospel, there are also personal and ministry ambitions that rise. As soon as we seek to appease these with accommodation and honour, more and more voices speak up with: "What about me? Why wasn't I asked to lead? "Why wasn't my name on the poster?" The focus shifts to finding the impossible balance where everyone is satisfied that they have been honoured and accommodated in an appropriate way. It's exhausting and requires great political skill to keep all the interests from flying apart.

Unity that is Christ centred is about lifting Him up together, not us seeking to be lifted up in front of our brothers and sisters. It requires dying to self, being willing to step up or step back, deeply listening to one another, and much prayer. It is forged with love and trust.

Knowing each other's hearts and trusting motives, even if actions or words seem off track, will keep us in unity when the pressure increases. Sustained revival requires a team, with daily meetings or perhaps multiple meetings a day, follow-up with new believers, maintaining prayer, deliverance ministry, taking care of finances, worship teams, and hospitality for visiting guests. Even custodial work gets taxed to the limits. Churches that might not be as involved, can still stand in unity with blessing what God is doing, encouragement, and prayer.

If a united team of pastors and leaders are walking together and no one is vying for prominence or needs to self-promote, this team can together sustain and steward a move of God.

Sustained Prayer

A frequent pitfall once revival begins is to neglect, rather than bolster, the place of fervent prayer. The temptation is that we are joyously overwhelmed with what is happening all around us, and we find it hard to prioritize a place of continued asking. If the answer is here, why keep crying out?!

In addition, revivals usually begin suddenly, and everyone is scrambling to keep up with the increase of all the spiritual activity, just trying to ride the wave without getting overwhelmed. Prayer can easily get crowded out.

But once revival is underway, there is even more need for prayer to keep it from falling into the flesh, into deception, or from cooling off. Charles Finney, in his classic volume, *Revival Lectures*, teaches at length about the things that cool down or even shut down the work of God in a revival. These primarily come down to pride, division, and other works of the flesh. The pressure and attention revival brings open up new opportunities for us to either press in deeper to God or fall into snares.

"Are you so foolish? After beginning by means of the Spirit, are you now trying to finish by means of the flesh?" Galatians 3:3

Prayer surely births revival, but it is just as necessary to sustain it and keep it from going off course.

The enemy of our souls is very active in a time of revival. He's is losing massive territory, as souls are won, as sin is repented of, and as reconciliation and healing flows. The demonic kingdom won't take these losses passively but will work at length to assault any weak area in the move of God or the key leaders involved. Boldly praying scripture and walking humbly are always our best defenses from warfare. It's what Jesus modeled.

So intercession must be an ongoing priority, which means bolstering this essential ministry through designating time, space, visibility, and the participation of primary leaders. It also means that secret prayer, like Pastor Bob gave himself to, should be encouraged to flourish in all believer's lives, even if it begins with baby steps.

An Empowered Body

Lastly, we can see sustaining revival requires the activation and empowerment of the priesthood of all believers.

"And he gave the apostles, the prophets, the evangelists, the shepherds and teachers, to equip the saints for the work of ministry, for building up the body of Christ, until we all attain to the unity of the faith and of the knowledge of the Son of God, to mature manhood, to the measure of the stature of the fullness of Christ." Ephesians 4:11–13

Unity holds us together, but the full diversity of gifts, and anointings need to be empowered to serve in all in times, but even more so in times of revival. The most obvious contrast is the way that revival flowed into many churches and then into many cities through both the Saskatoon Revival and the Toronto Blessing, compared with Henry Alline who laboured without an effective team surrounding him, leading to the revival waning when his health failed.

In Toronto and Saskatoon, there was beautiful unity in a leadership level, but it didn't stop there. Long nights were spent counseling and praying with those under the dealings of God in Saskatoon, requiring many labourers, not just pastors. Teams commissioned to carry the fire to other cities, provinces and nations were sent out of Saskatoon's hub, and many of these labourers were laymen. In Toronto, ministry teams in the same way, sacrificially served those that were being transformed by God's love.

So as we contend for national revival through prayer, let's also prepare by building authentic heart-level unity and proactively welcome a move of God with action. It might mean learning a new skill, or polishing up an old one so we can serve effectively.

A great revival will require great humility, servant-hearts and love beyond what we have known. We each have been placed alongside others, like living stones built together to form a temple, a container for His presence. Let's love the whole body of Christ but discern which "stones" the Lord has positioned us beside and wholeheartedly invest ourselves in these relationships.

Together, we can help each other keep the vision of the expansiveness and beauty of the kingdom of God before us. We all have our part and our passion, but it's so much bigger than any of us. It's about the life of heaven bursting forth and the power of that resurrection radically reforming the kingdoms of this world.

"Then the seventh angel blew his trumpet, and there were loud voices in heaven, saying, The kingdom of the world has become the kingdom of our Lord and of his Christ, and he shall reign forever and ever.'"
Revelation 11:15

Hope Again

This book began with a revival that broke out under Henry Alline's preaching in 1776, and concluded with the more recent Toronto Blessing Revival that began in January 1994. You may have noticed a pattern through the pages as we looked at some of the most significant revivals God has poured out in Canada. They are getting more frequent. Like great birth pains of a national spiritual labour, the contractions are consistent and closer and closer together. In fact, in the last century, the outbreak of revival has been averaging about every twenty-one years.

This means we are quite possibly due for another outpouring. How then shall we respond?

I pray that these stories have not just been a historical education or review for you, nor have they just added to your awareness of the Canadian journey. I pray, rather, that there has been a rise of faith and fire in your own heart as you recognize how invested and close God has been to this nation. I pray that the way He's heard the prayers of our forefathers, how He's seen their labours and been moved by their humility, repentance and faith, has become intensely real to you. But even more than that, I pray that greater revelation of how He's more than willing to move among us, in even more wonderful ways has lifted your faith and vision. He's willing to respond to us. He's been waiting for this hour.

Perhaps disappointment has made even the idea of revival painful for you. Perhaps you've given much prayer to revival and once passionately believed, yet never saw what you believed for. What you were told was imminent didn't come to pass. Through the lenses of disappointment, the fresh declarations of revival coming may seem hollow and foolish. Maybe the term *revival* has been thrown around too freely, and what you experienced in the name of revival was full of flesh and unbiblical excess, leaving you confused and heartbroken.

Maybe overenthusiastic prophetic words, declaring that revival is about to break out here or there, which never transpired, have created distrust and a reticence to listen to the prophetic voice again.

Wherever you've been, however difficult the journey has become, authentic revivals bring thousands, hundreds of thousands, and even millions of souls into the kingdom. Homes and marriages are restored, and demons are cast out. Healings are frequent, and burnt-out leaders are refreshed and refired. The Church gets cleansed, renewed in love for Jesus, and set on fire with zealous purpose. God comes near.

Revival is still what we long for.

All through the scriptures are stories of barren women miraculously conceiving, (even when they were well beyond childbearing years) and giving birth to nation changers.

Sarai, Sarah—Mother of Isaac
"Sarai was barren; she had no child." Genesis 11:30

"By faith even Sarah herself received ability to conceive, even beyond the proper time of life, since she considered Him faithful who had promised." Hebrews 11:11

Rebekah—Mother of Jacob
"And Isaac prayed to the LORD for his wife, because she was barren. And the LORD granted his prayer, and Rebekah his wife conceived." Genesis 25:21

Rachel—Mother of Joseph
"Now the LORD saw that Leah was unloved, and He opened her womb, but Rachel was barren.
Now when Rachel saw that she bore Jacob no children, she became jealous of her sister; and she said to Jacob, 'Give me children, or else I die.'" Gen 29:31, 30:1

Samson's Mother
"There was a certain man of Zorah, of the family of the Danites, whose name was Manoah; and his wife was barren and had borne no children. Then the angel of the LORD appeared to the woman and said to her, 'Behold now, you are barren and have borne no children, but you shall conceive and give birth to a son.'" Judges 13:2,3

Hannah—Mother of Samuel
"But to Hannah he gave a double portion, because he loved her, though the LORD had closed her womb. And her rival used to provoke her grievously to irritate her, because the LORD had closed her womb. So it went on year by year. As often as she went up to the house of the LORD, she used to provoke her. Therefore Hannah wept and would not eat." 1Samuel 1:5–7

Elizabeth—Mother of John the Baptist
"But the angel said to him, 'Do not be afraid, Zacharias, for your petition has been heard, and your wife Elizabeth will bear you a son, and you will give him the name John." Luke 1:13

Some of these women had given up on having children, and some tried to make it happen in other ways. Still others, like Hannah, were intensely provoked and went to prayer and fasting. God uses barrenness to stir a profound, unrelenting desire for life, be it natural or spiritual.

We have before us the precious mantles of our forefathers—things they apprehended in the spirit, which we can treasure and walk in as well. But it's a walk that begins with faith and desire. Do we care enough and want an explosion of spiritual life around us enough to go after God? Do we believe that He is the rewarder of those that will earnestly seek him?

There is already a growing company of people who will believe, who will labour and pray for revival like it is the child they don't yet have but so deeply long for. This company is not faultless, but it's growing in passion, maturing in prayer, pouring out its heart in worship, and seeking to always be ready to share the gospel. Will you join these burning ones that are rising up, even if you've been heartsick with disappointment before?

I believe a national company, a remnant of those who will give themselves to this labour in the Spirit, who will unite in one heart and put everything they can into contending for revival to sweep the nation - will be enough to tip the bowls. Think back to our stories. There weren't many in prayer at the front end of each revival. But those that carried this burden were unrelenting in prayer, fasting, and obedience.

If you are sensing God is recruiting you for this revival mandate that is being offered to this generation, invite Him now to use you. Ask Him for the mantle of prayer and fasting that the Sharon Bible School or Frank Small walked in. Ask Him for the faith of Charles Price and the perseverance of Bill McLeod.

If we rise up together and pursue this holy opportunity—determined that, in the same way revival is roaring through the body of Christ in other nations, it will not pass us by—it will also crash powerfully upon our shores.

If we rise up, this next chapter, now a blank page, will surely contain a glorious story of a new revival mantle in our nation. Who will stand in the gap and call it into being? History is waiting for an intercessor.

About the Author

Sara Maynard is the founder and director of Redleaf Prayer Ministries. She has been leading intercession both in the Vancouver area and nationally in Canada for nearly 20 years, with a continual hunger for revival. After Bible school and working in a youth evangelism ministry in the US, she married her best friend Mike, and built a financial planning practice in downtown Vancouver. She returned to full-time ministry in 2000 as a part of the founding team and then director, of Canada's first House of Prayer (VHOP). In 2003 the Lord called her to launch a more nationally focused intercessory ministry and so, Redleaf Prayer was born.

As the director of Redleaf, Sara invests most of her focus into the Red Leaf House of Prayer, keeping it growing and filled with faith, vision, and the spirit of prayer. However, she also loves to carve time out to encourage and coach other prayer ministries that are emerging, particularly those that are mobilizing the younger generation. She travels frequently, teaching and equipping on prayer and revival, activating and calling the Church to the place of effective, joyful, intercession.

Sara and Mike have been married for 32 years and have three sons, who have married exceptional women and with them, are whole-heartedly serving God.

To follow Sara on Twitter: @SaraMaynard1
For booking Sara to speak: info@redleafprayer.org

About Redleaf Prayer Ministries

RLHOP: The Red Leaf House of Prayer is a nation-wide house of prayer for Canada that meets to pray in online video conference calls. Its primary mandate is to unite prayer for nation-wide revival and harvest and to that end is working toward establishing a hundred fiery, faith-filled, Bible-based, weekly prayer meetings within the house of prayer that anyone in Canada who loves Jesus can participate in. Prayer missionaries are a key part of RLHOP and serve in the house of prayer anywhere from fifteen to forty hours a week. For those with a passion for revival, this is an excellent ministry opportunity. To register to join a prayer meeting or to find out more about becoming a missionary, check out the website:
rlhop.ca

Equipping: Redleaf is committed to equipping. They hold regular on-line training courses, summer internships, and Sara frequently travels to teach at schools of intercession held by either one, or a group, of like-minded churches. Please inquire at the main ministry website if this is of interest to you:
redleafprayer.org

Prayer Events and Initiatives: As God leads, Redleaf will be involved with, or give leadership to, national calls to prayer, rallies, strategic prayer campaigns and conferences.

Ears2Hear Council

In 2006, Redleaf initiated a network of Canadian prayer leaders, which has grown into the Ears2Hear Council, a group of over sixty leaders from many denominations, generations, and regions of Canada, walking together. The Council meets annually for a summit, and monthly by video conferencing to share what God is saying and doing across the nation, to pray, and to encourage each other. Each month, the most significant highlights of these national meetings are distilled into prayer points and distributed widely through an email newsletter. To sign up for this newsletter, or to read past archives please go online to:

ears2hear.ca.

Notes

[1] Mt 11:12 *Scripture is taken from GOD'S WORD®, © 1995 God's Word to the Nations. Used by permission of Baker Publishing Group.*

[2] Henry Alline, *The Life and Journal of the Mr. Rev. Henry Alline*, (Boston: Gillbert & Dean, 1806), 34

[3] G. A. Rawlyk *The Canada Fire: Radical Evangelicalism in British North America 1775–1812*, (Montreal:McGill-Queen's University Press, 1994), 2, 5

[4] Alline, *Life and Journal*, 59

[5] Ibid.

[6] "Revival Library, Henry Alline:1748—1784", accessed September 6, 2013, http://www.revival-library.org/pensketches/revivalists/allinej.html

[7] Jack Bumsted, "The Father of the New Lights: Henry Alline", in *Canada Portraits of Faith*, Michael Clarke, (Chilliwack:Reel to Reel, 1998), 29

[8] Henry Alline, *New Light Letters and Songs*, editor George Rawlyk, (Hantsport, NS: Lancelot Press, 1983),189

[9] Gerald Procee, "Revivals in North America: The Hamilton, Ontario, Canada Revival of 1857", accessed July 12, 2014, http://reformedresource.net/index.php/worldviews/the-hand-of-god-in-histroy/124-revivals-in-north-america-the-hamilton-ontario-canada-revival-of-1857.html

[10] Ibid.

[11] Earle Cairns, *An Endless Line of Splendor: Revivals and Their Leaders From the Great Awakening to the Present*, (Wheaton:Tyndale,1986),148

[12] "Revivals in North America"

[13] Ibid

[14] Daina Doucet, "The Day When Hamilton Changed the World", originally published in *The Beacon*, July/Aug 2007

[15] Ibid

[16] Fred Smith, "Christian Humility", Leadership Journal, Winter 1984, accessed July 18, 2014, http://www.christianitytoday.com/le/1984/winter/84l1118.html

Notes

[17] Toronto Daily Mail and Empire, as quoted by Kevin Kee— "The Heavenly Railroad: John Hunter, 1856—1919", *Canada Portraits of Faith*, Michael Clarke, (Chilliwack:Reel to Reel, 1998), 83

[18] Oswald J. Smith, *The Passion for Souls*, (London: Marshall, Morgan and Scott, 1950), 71

[19] Kee, "John Hunter", 83

[20] Psalms 72:8

[21] Isaiah 6:5

[22] "Or do you presume on the riches of his kindness and forbearance and patience, not knowing that God's kindness is meant to lead you to repentance?" Romans 2:4

[23] Robert Larden, *Our Apostolic Heritage: An Official History of the Apostolic Church of Pentecost of Canada Incorporated*, (Canada: ACOP, 1971),28

[24] Stanley Burgess and Eduard van der Mass, *The New International Dictionary of Pentecostal and Charismatic Movements* (Grand Rapids: Zondervan, 2002),1075

[25] Larden, *Apostolic Heritage*, 34

[26] Ibid., 57

[27] Ibid., 58

[28] Ibid., 57

[29] Frank Ewart, *"The Phenomenon of Pentecost"*, (Houston, Tx:Herald Publishing House) Chapter 16.

[30] Ibid., 76

[31] Jn 12:24

[32] *Vancouver Province*, May 2, 1923

[33] Robert K Burkinshaw, *Pilgrims in Lotus Land: Conservative Protestantism in British Columbia, 1917- 1981*, (Montreal: McGill-Queen's University Press, 1995), 106

[34] *The Later Rain Evangel*, (August 1923), 11

[35] Burkinshaw, *Pilgrims in Lotusland*, 110

[36] The majority of this chapter has come directly from my previous book: *Renew it in our Day: The Forgotten Westcoast Revival of 1923*, (Self Published, 2005)

[37] "For faith comes by hearing, and hearing by the word of God" Romans 10:17

[38] Job 13:15

[39] Richard Riss, *A Survey of 20th Century Revival Movements in North America*, (Peabody, Mass.: Hendrickson,1988), 106

[40] Reg Layzell, *Unto Perfection: A Sequel to the Pastor's Pen*, (Washington: The Kings Temple, 1979), 4

[41] Ernest Hawtin, *How this Revival Began*, p 3 as quoted by Richard Riss, *The Latter Rain Movement of 1948 and the Mid-Twentieth Century Evangelical Awakening*, (M.C.S. Thesis, Regent College, April, 1979), 77

[42] *The Sharon Star*, (May 1952) p 3 as quoted by Richard Riss, *The Later Rain Movement of 1948*, 86–87

[43] Hawtin, *How this Revival Began*, quoted by Richard Riss, 3

[44] Violet Kiteley, "Remembering the Latter Rain", *Charisma Magazine*, accessed May 19, 2014, http://www.charismamag.com/spirit/devotionals/daily-breakthroughs?view=article&id=9494:remembering-the-latter-rain&catid=24

[45] Reg Layzell, *Unto Perfection*, 17–19

[46] Riss, *20th Century Revival Movements*, 115

[47] Jonas Clark, "The Latter Rain Revival, Reg Layzell: Apostle of the Latter Rain", *The Voice Magazine*, accessed May 19, 2014, http://www.thevoicemagazine.com/latterrain_reg_Layzell.htm

[48] Riss, *20th Century Revival Movements*, 116

[49] Ibid.

[50] We recommend: The Rewards of Fasting by Mike Bickle, Forerunner Books, 2005/ A Hunger for God by John Piper, Crossway Books, 1997/ Hidden Power of Prayer and Fasting by Mahesh Chavda, Destiny Image, 1998

[51] NHOP—National House of Prayer, a wonderful Canadian ministry, based in Ottawa, focused on praying for righteousness in Parliament and for governmental leaders.

[52] Larry Eskridge, *God's Forever Family: the Jesus Movement in America*, (New York: Oxford University Press, 2013)

[53] Beth Carson, *Pastor Bob: A Statesman of Prayer for Canada*, (Belleville, ON: Guardian, 2003), 184

[54] Ibid.

[55] Ibid., 186

[56] Riss, *20th Century Revival Movements*, 148

[57] Carson, *Pastor Bob*, 200

[58] Ibid.

[59] Ibid.

[60] Henry Blackaby and Claude King, *Experiencing God*, (Nashville: Lifeway Press, 1990), 15

[61] As recounted by Bill McLeod

[62] Kurt Koch, *Revival Fires in Canada* (West Germany: Ev. Verlag, 1973), 26

[63] As recounted by Bill McLeod, in a video interview

[64] ibid.

[65] ibid.

[66] Koch, *Revival Fires*, 27

[67] The Alliance in Saskatoon, accessed October 3, 2013, http://www.collegeofprayer.ca/saskatoon/content/revival.html

[68] Koch, *Revival Fires*, 38

[69] Ibid., 27

[70] Main source of the content of this chapter: Video interviews with Pastor Bill McLeod, accessed Sept 5–10, 2013 https://www.youtube.com/watch?v=K-HJFtQvIec

[71] Carins, *An Endless Line of Splendor*, 230

[72] Henry Blackaby, "Revival Scenes", *Revival Commentary, v. 1, n. 1.*

[73] Luke 18

[74] An excellent resource on the prophetic is Stacey Campbell's book Ecstatic Prophecy, published by Chosen Books, 2008.

[75] James 4:6

[76] John Arnott, *Experience the Blessing*, (Ventura: Renew Books, 2000) 10

[77] "Catch the Fire History", accessed August 10, 2014, http://www.catchthefire.com/About/History

[78] Jerry Steingard and John Arnott, *From Here to the Nations: The Story of the Toronto Blessing*, (Toronto: Catch the Fire Books, 2014), excerpt from his book emailed to author, November 29, 2014

[79] Global Awakening–Randy Clark, accessed August 14, 2014, http://globalawakening.com/home/speakers/randy-clark

[80] Steingard, *From Here to the Nations*

[81] Isaiah 33:14

[82] When I Survey the Wondrous Cross by Isaac Watts—Public Domain